THE
LEADERSHIP
PARADOX

Becoming Great Through Service

GEORGE M. FLATTERY, ED.D.

Thank you, Pastor Serbin, for your ministry and support.

George M. Flattery

Network211

Springfield, Missouri

www.network211.com

Network211 (GMF) Edition
Springfield, MO USA
www.network211.com

THE LEADERSHIP PARADOX:
Becoming Great Through Service

ISBN: Network211 (GMF) Paperback Edition: 978-0-9851788-5-7

CONTENTS

FOREWORD

I have had the privilege of knowing Dr. George (as we affectionately call him) since 1980. There are many superlatives I could use to describe him—*visionary, steward, friend,* and *colleague* come quickly to mind. Still other words describe his character—*faithful, tenacious, insightful,* and *trustworthy,* among many others.

In this context, the word *leader* is appropriate. With the myriad of works on leadership, Dr. George exemplifies great leadership on multiple levels. His leadership can be demonstrated on a macro level by the organizations he founded and/or led (such as ICI, Global University, and Network211) and his interactions with denominational leadership, accrediting associations, and pedagogical leadership across the world spectrum. He also exemplifies leadership on a more personal level with his staff members and his own family.

This book presents tried, positive, and successful leadership principles with illustrative material to make it applicable and practical. I recommend it to further develop the leader in all of us.

Greg Mundis, D.Min.

Executive Director
Assemblies of God World Missions

INTRODUCTION

In the summer of 1973, the story in Matthew 20:20-28 about becoming great by being a servant captured my attention. I was sitting on our sofa in our apartment in Brussels, Belgium, reading this story when it hit me. Matthew's story, it seemed to me, deals with many important leadership issues. We had been in Brussels just over one year and were attempting to further establish and develop the worldwide ministry of International Correspondence Institute (ICI) which became ICI University and then Global University. As president of ICI, I was at times confronted with issues such as those raised in this story.

When I read Matthew's story, I was teaching a class each Sunday at Christian Center, a newly planted international church. I developed ten lessons for this class based on this story which I taught in August and September of 1973. Since then, I have taught this ten-lesson series in various places around the world. Now, these lessons have become chapters in this book along with two chapters that I have added. All of the chapters deal with leadership issues with an emphasis on servant leadership. The twelfth chapter is devoted to a consideration of how to serve.

Jesus drew a sharp contrast between rulers that stress authority and leaders that emphasize service. Through the use of two triangles, we can contrast the ruler and his authority with the servant leader. To illustrate the ruler, draw a triangle with one angle, the apex, at the top. Then put the ruler, the person regarded as great, on the apex and the people being led below. The bottom horizontal line represents the people. Jesus turns the triangle upside down. To illustrate His approach to the servant leader, draw an inverted triangle with the single angle at the bottom. Then put the servant, the truly great person, on this angle and the people above. The horizontal line, which is now at the top, signifies the people being served.

The overarching message of the story in Matthew is that service is the indispensable element in great leadership. While making this point, Jesus addressed His remarks to whoever would be great and whoever would be first. Paradoxically, the one who wants to be great must be the servant of all and the one who wants to be first must be the slave. By implication, the paradox of leadership is that leaders become great through service. Jesus does not rebuke the desire to be great or even to be first, but He shows the way. Although many servant leaders have authority, service, not authority, has the priority.

Over the years, I have sought to apply the leadership principles based on Matthew's story to the organizations that I served. We looked upon these principles as guiding ideals, and we had many opportunities to apply the message of this story to our work. Although we did not make Matthew's story a part of the constitutions and bylaws of these organizations, we treated it as such. This story tells all ministries, as well as secular businesses, the best way to pursue their goals.

With regard to the story, Jesus and the disciples were on the way to Jerusalem. He had already told them three times in Matthew's gospel that He was facing death and resurrection in Jerusalem (Matt. 16:21-23; 17:22-23; and 20:17-19). However, it is obvious that the disciples still had not fully understood the implications of what He said.

In spite of all these warnings, the attention of the disciples was focused on their own leadership roles. Two of the disciples, James and John, wanted positions of honor very much in the way of the world as it existed at that time. They seemed to be interested in power, prestige, glory, and fame instead of the best interests of Christ's kingdom, not grasping what His kingdom was all about. The death and resurrection of Christ would introduce a totally new order, one in which greatness and leadership are based on service rather than power.

Both Matthew and Mark present this leadership story (Matt. 20:20-28; Mark 10:35-45). This book is based on Matthew's version with supplemental information added from Mark. The two accounts are different at a couple of points that we will discuss when we deal with the relevant verses. With this as background, here is the story as Matthew tells it:

> ²⁰Then the mother of the sons of Zebedee came to Jesus with her sons, bowing down and making a request of Him.
> ²¹And He said to her, "What do you wish?"
> She said to Him, "Command that in Your kingdom these two sons of mine may sit one on Your right and one on Your left."
> ²²But Jesus answered, "You do not know what you are asking. Are you able to drink the cup that I am about to drink?" They said to Him, "We are able."
> ²³He said to them, "My cup you shall drink; but to sit on My right and on *My* left, this is not Mine to give, but it is for those for whom it has been prepared by My Father."

²⁴And hearing *this*, the ten became indignant with the two brothers.

²⁵But Jesus called them to Himself and said, "You know that the rulers of the Gentiles lord it over them, and *their* great men exercise authority over them.

²⁶It is not this way among you, but whoever wishes to become great among you shall be your servant.

²⁷and whoever wishes to be first among you shall be your slave;

²⁸just as the Son of Man did not come to be served, but to serve, and to give His life a ransom for many."

This story impacts both individuals and organizations. Jesus addressed His remarks to "whoever wishes to become great." Jesus called them as individuals to be servants. As servant leaders, they will have a huge impact on the groups they lead. The impact of an individual is seen by Ralph Waldo Emerson when he says, "Every great institution is the lengthened shadow of a single man. His character determines the character of the organization" (thinkexist.com). Many churches are known as much or more by the name of the pastor as by the name of the church. The same is true of many businesses and their leaders, especially when the leaders own the businesses.

Organizations enter the picture because their leaders often want their organizations to be great. In fact, many entities expressly state that becoming the best in their field is their objective. Jesus does not explicitly address organizations and their desire to be great or first. However, the fact that true greatness lies in service is true for organizations also. Therefore, many of the principles in this book apply both to organizations and institutions becoming great as well as to individuals.

Matthew's story has inspired both secular and Christian leaders everywhere. It is one of the main biblical sources for what has become known as servant leadership. Ever since Matthew and Mark recorded the story, it has been a blessing to church leaders everywhere. Today, many secular leaders, as well as church leaders, have adopted the philosophy of leading through service.

Preview of the Chapters

This is a very powerful story which deals with basic leadership issues. In my discussion of the issues raised by the story, I will not limit myself to an exposition of the text, but we will study the text verse-by-verse. In each chapter, we will bring in additional material from other sources. I will not read the additional material into the text, but I also will not limit my comments to what the text says. The text raises the topics, and I deal with the topics. Here is a short description of each chapter.

Chapter one is titled "What Leadership Is." The entire passage in Matthew (20:20-28), especially verses 25-28, provide the background for this chapter. In this chapter, I present the need for leaders and give various definitions of leadership, including my own. Then I discuss the relationship of service and greatness with an emphasis on service as the indispensable quality of both secular and Christian servant leadership.

Verses 20 and 21 suggest the topic for chapter two which is "The Desire to Lead." The mother of James and John asked Jesus to command that they sit on his right hand and His left hand in His Kingdom. This chapter presents my comments on the desired positions and what it meant to sit in these honored seats. Following this, I discuss the reaction and reply of Jesus, both giving comments on when it is right and when it is wrong to want to lead and on the results of leadership through service.

The third chapter deals with "The Price of Leadership." This issue is raised when Jesus identifies the cost he will pay as the "cup" that He will drink (verse 22a) and the "baptism" that He will experience (verse 23a KJV and Mark 10:38). In His response, Christ spoke about the cost that the disciples would pay. With this as a starting point, I discuss twelve costs that leaders may face as they serve and then turn to the topic of meeting the challenge.

Chapter four is a study of "The Leader's Confidence." Verse 22b gives rise to this subject. Here, Matthew quotes James and John as saying, "We are able." We will include a look at both the positive and negative aspects of the leader's confidence and then present some thoughts on mitigating extremes. Next I will speak about placing our full confidence in Christ. This will lead to some thoughts on developing confidence with Moses as an example.

In chapter five, we will study "The Leader's Destiny." This chapter is based on verse 23 where Jesus indicates that being seated at His right and left hands is determined by the Father. This raises issues that have to do with destiny. Although man's finite mind cannot fully reconcile free will and God's sovereignty, this chapter provides some practical action suggestions. I present my view of controlled freedom in which man can exercise free will within God's control. Next, I apply this view to positions of leadership and to greatness, followed by some ideas on a course of action.

Matthew tells us in verse 24 that ten of the disciples became indignant with James and John. Sooner or later, as chapter six explains, most leaders are confronted with upset co-workers. Thus, I have titled chapter six "Indignant Colleagues," where I write about three prospective leaders, James and John and Joseph, and then write about the colleagues of James and John and the brothers of Joseph. I include a section on pathways to leadership, followed by some suggestions on action principles.

The subject of chapter seven is "The Leader's Authority." This chapter keys on verse 25 which deals with the role of authority. I describe how Jesus deals with the abuse of authority, using "Gentile" leadership as an example. Next, I discuss the necessity of authority, including a section on management using Moses in Exodus 18:13-26 as an example. The story of Moses opens up a discussion of ten aspects of management. Next, I deal with the right use of authority. Servant leaders need to have a proper perspective concerning authority and act appropriately.

In chapter eight, my subject is "The Hazards of Leadership." There are many hazards to leadership, including the abuse of power (verse 25). Listing this pitfall raises the possibility of others. Our attention in this chapter is focused on compromise and manipulation. Compromise is bad when ethical positions are waived, but it can be good when ethical principles are not involved. Manipulation, in a figurative sense, is the attempt to gain something by unfair means. Leaders face many potential pitfalls and must be diligent to avoid them.

Chapter nine deals with verses 26-27 where we come to the very heart of the Matthew story. The chapter is about "Leading Through Service." Jesus addresses his comments to "whoever wishes to become great" and "whoever wishes to be first." Here, we begin by recalling the types of leaders from chapter one. This is followed by a discussion of meeting the needs of people. Jesus clearly came to meet needs with emphasis on the real needs. We conclude this chapter with comments on ways to lead through service.

The subject of chapter ten is "A Ransom for Many." In this chapter, we emphasize that Jesus came to minister to people around Him and, while He did not come to be ministered to, the disciples on their own initiative ministered to Him. Next, we discuss what it means that Jesus came to give His life as a "ransom" for many and to whom, if anyone, the ransom was paid. Finally, we write about how we should act as followers of Christ. We cannot be a ransom in the sense that Christ was, but we can pay the price of being witnesses to the entire world.

The topic of chapter eleven is "The Call of God to Serve." Verses 21, 23, 26, and 27 are especially relevant to this subject. The term "call of God" has broader meanings, but our concern here is our call to serve. Therefore, I discuss the relationship between the desire to lead and the call of God to serve, consider the needs people have and His call to serve by meeting these needs, and present several Biblical examples of God calling His servants. Then I deal with how we hear God calling. The ways we hear God call are also ways to find the will of God.

This final chapter deals with "How to Serve." The main point Jesus proclaimed in the Matthew story is that "whoever wishes to be great among you shall be your servant" (verse 26). This brings into focus our topic for this chapter. In the organizations that I served with over many years, our goal and ideal was to serve. The principles presented tell us how we can lead by serving. I discuss general principles of leadership, how to work with top leaders, how to work with other organizations, how to work with staff, and some guidelines for self-discipline.

The Context

Over six years before the Matthew story captured my attention, I proposed the formation of International Correspondence Institute (ICI) to the Foreign Missions Department (FMD) of the General Council of the Assemblies of God. This department is now known as Assemblies of God World Missions (AGWM). Much later, in 1997, with the approval of AGWM, I founded the global Internet ministry named Network211. A brief description of these ministries will shed light on the context in which we sought to apply leadership principles. These ministries were an experiential workshop.

ICI was formed in 1967 and became known as ICI University in 1993. In 1999, Berean University and ICI University united to become Global University. Global University is a distance education school that works worldwide through its network of offices in 156 countries. The network also includes schools of the University under local names. Additionally, it has working agreements with many resident Bible schools. Global University is committed to evangelism, discipleship, and training at all levels from non-credit training up through doctoral programs. It is accredited by the Higher Learning Commission in the United States.

Network211, which started as Global Colleagues, is a global ministry of evangelism and discipleship via the Internet. Using this means, it presents the gospel to millions of people from nearly every country in the world. It has hundreds of "connectors" who interact with people who write to us to help them grow in Christ. In addition, it has an online church called Global Christian Center and a social media site named Global Friend Link. We work with a network of churches through targeted evangelism campaigns and by syndicating content to their web sites.

As past president of Global University, under its different names, and Network211, I worked with many of the leaders of the Assemblies of God at home and abroad. Consequently, I had the opportunity to observe their leadership up close for several decades. Their examples were instructive for me as I sought to follow good leadership principles. Hopefully, some of what I learned from them is reflected in the chapters in this book. I wish to sincerely thank all of these leaders for their leadership, their moral support of our efforts, and their strong commitment to the advancement of the Kingdom of God.

In addition, Global University and Network211 provided me with a great opportunity to work together with hundreds of staff members on a global scale. Many of them were outstanding leaders in their own right. With regard to our central office, many secular and church visitors told us that they were surprised by the commitment and passion manifested by our entire staff. With profound gratitude, I thank all of these co-workers and our colleagues worldwide for their wisdom and service.

About this Book

A few comments about this book may be helpful to you in understanding the leadership context of my remarks. Therefore, I would call your attention to the following points:

First, it is not my purpose to present a survey of the latest literature on leadership. It is my desire to present information that has had a positive impact on me and my service roles over the decades. Consequently, some of the references in this revised version are older, while others are more recent. The older sources are still valid and acquaint the reader with leadership approaches that form a basis of much of what is said today. When you consider the older sources and the more recent, you can see trends clearly emerging. For example, a strong trend is the emphasis on servant leadership.

Second, it is my purpose to write about leading through service. What Jesus says lets us know that service is the indispensable factor in greatness and in great leadership. I have used the term "indispensable" repeatedly. There are synonyms such as absolutely necessary, essential, requisite, and required, but indispensable seems to me to be more precise. Therefore, at the risk of being repetitive, I have used this term throughout this book.

Third, my point in this book is not to say that service is the only important aspect of leadership. There are other leadership elements. For example, both vision and good management are very important in the leadership of any church or organization. In my view, we should not overlook these factors, but rather we should consider them as ways to serve. We serve the people well when we have vision and manage well. So we need to consider these characteristics and how they relate to service.

Fourth, as stated above, this book was a series of lessons that I have taught since 1973. This revised version is in book form, but I have retained the outline so that a teacher can easily use it in a classroom setting. A word about the form of the outline in each chapter should be helpful. The major parts of each chapter are identified by centered headings. Under each centered heading are the relevant points identified as first, second, third, and successive numbers. Then, under each of these points are sub-points including *one*, *two*, *three*, *four*, and so on. The terms "first" and "one" designate different levels of content. Hopefully, the outlines in the chapters will be helpful to both the reader and anyone who teaches from this book.

Fifth, unless otherwise stated, all the Scriptures in this book are quoted from the New American Standard Bible, 1995 version (NASB95). Other versions cited are the New International Version, the King James Version, the New English Bible, and the version by George M. Lamsa.

Acknowledgements

Sincere thanks go to several people who helped me with the production of this book. James E. Richardson, Ph.D., skilfully edited my work. He is the associate dean of the Graduate School of Theology and director of doctoral studies for Global University. Russ Langford, who is the director of library services at Global University, very kindly assisted me in my research. A director of content at Network211, James Cole-Rous, read my manuscript and made helpful suggestions. J. David Ford and his firm develop the graphics for the cover. My grandson Seth Flattery assisted by posting my chapters on the Internet. I greatly appreciate the work that each of these persons has done.

Many thanks to our sons, George and Mark, who have interacted with me for many years regarding leadership principles. George and Debbie Flattery were missionaries to France and planted a church in Paris. After this, they served as lead pastors in the United States for 27 years. Now, they are returning to France to plant an English-speaking international church. Mark Flattery has served as a missionary for twenty-five years. He served in Tanzania, East Africa, and then as Area Director for AGWM in Pacific Oceania. An AGWM Area Director is the lead person in a given geographical area. Currently he is serving as president of Network211.

Finally, I wish to thank my wife, Esther, who worked with me throughout our ministry. She has by nature promoted good will and inspiration among all of our team members. Her understanding of people and rapport with them has been a major positive element in our work. Also, her companionship with me personally has been a huge blessing.

George M. Flattery

Chancellor, Global University
Founder, Network211

CHAPTER ONE

WHAT LEADERSHIP IS

Introduction

As Matthew tells the story, the mother of James and John, accompanied by them, came to Jesus with a request. She asked Jesus to command that her sons would sit on His right hand and left hand in His kingdom. Mark, in his gospel, records only that James and John made the request (Mark 10:35). Obviously, James and John were involved with their mother in presenting the request.

The reply of Jesus and His interaction with the disciples raised several key issues concerning greatness and leadership. Jesus deals with these issues and then presents His overarching teaching on the true nature of servant leadership. He makes it very clear that the indispensable element is service. The term *leadership* is used by many people to identify other ways to lead, but the servant leader puts the highest priority on meeting the needs of the people he serves.

The entire story, as related by Matthew and Mark, forms the background for all the chapters in this book, including this one on what leadership is. Keeping the whole story in mind, we will study Matthew's version verse-by-verse and discuss the issues that are raised. To facilitate this approach, I have included Matthew's story at the beginning of each chapter. According to Matthew 20:20-28, here is what happened:

> ²⁰Then the mother of the sons of Zebedee came to Jesus with her sons, bowing down and making a request of Him.
>
> ²¹And He said to her, "What do you wish?"
> She said to Him, "Command that in Your kingdom these two sons of mine may sit one on Your right and one on Your left."
>
> ²²But Jesus answered, "You do not know what you are asking. Are you able to drink the cup that I am about to drink?" They said to Him, "We are able."
>
> ²³He said to them, "My cup you shall drink; but to sit on My right and on *My* left, this is not Mine to give, but it is for those for whom it has been prepared by My Father."
>
> ²⁴And hearing *this*, the ten became indignant with the two brothers.

²⁵But Jesus called them to Himself and said, "You know that the rulers of the Gentiles lord it over them, and *their* great men exercise authority over them.

²⁶It is not this way among you, but whoever wishes to become great among you shall be your servant.

²⁷and whoever wishes to be first among you shall be your slave;

²⁸just as the Son of Man did not come to be served, but to serve, and to give His life a ransom for many."

With this story in mind, we will devote this chapter to a discussion of the need for leadership, what leadership is, and service as the indispensable factor in greatness and servant leadership.

The Need for Leaders

Over the past several decades, many books, articles, and ministries have dealt with the subject of leadership. This has been a very popular topic. Many, if not all, colleges, universities, and seminaries offer courses in leadership. Undoubtedly, this is due to the very great need that there is for leaders. As we think about this need, we will discuss our enormous task, the challenges that we face, and the demand for leaders.

First, we have been given an enormous task. Christ has commanded us to "preach the gospel to all creation" (Mark 16:15) and to "make disciples of all the nations" (Matt. 28:19). Moreover, God has assigned us the task of "equipping of the saints for the work of service, to the building up of the body of Christ" (Eph. 4:12). In addition, meeting the needs of the poor and the suffering is an important concern. When Jesus stated His mission, He included meeting the needs of those who are suffering spiritually, physically, and materially (Luke 4:18-19).

Many Christian organizations include these elements in their vision and mission statements. For example, I would cite the Assemblies of God World Missions (AGWM) organization with which I have served as a global missionary for several decades. The web site of AGWM presents its fourfold mission statement as follows:

- Reach. "We reach the spiritually lost with the message of Jesus Christ in all the world through every available means."
- Plant. "We plant churches in 255 countries, territories, and provinces following the New Testament pattern."
- Train. "We train leaders throughout the world to proclaim the message of Jesus Christ to their own people and to other nations."

- Serve. "We serve poor and suffering people with the compassion of Christ and invite them to become His followers."

These tasks engage the efforts of thousands of people throughout the world. Multitudes are at work in their own countries. In addition, thousands of people are going from their home countries to other countries to minister. They are going "from all nations to all nations."

Second, we are confronted with many challenges in completing the task. We must work in many languages, in a great variety of cultures, in difficult climates, with limited funds, with too few people, and many more. At least some of these challenges face every leader who seeks to accomplish the tasks just named. To accept a leadership role is to take on the challenges of the task.

Today, one of our most difficult challenges is to present Christ in the midst of many false ideologies, agnostic or atheistic philosophies, and strange doctrines. In our nation, as well as in many others, the truths of the gospel are under fire as never before. However, the challenge of preaching and preserving the truth is not new. This was one of Paul's main concerns. For example, his two epistles to Timothy emphasize this concern. He asked Timothy to take a leadership role in preserving the truth, making this comment (2 Tim. 2:2): "The things which you have heard from me in the presence of many witnesses, entrust these to faithful men who will be able to teach others also."

We may call these challenges either problems or opportunities. Either way, we must trust God for the solutions and keep advancing. The mountains must become as molehills as we follow the Lord. We must pray that the Lord, with His power in mind, will give us the right perspective.

Third, all these challenges demand leaders. Without leaders, the church languishes. Chaos, inefficiency, and aimlessness prevail. Moreover, the commands of Christ go unfulfilled. With leaders, goals are set, people are united, work progresses, and Christ's commands are fulfilled.

Fourth, the challenges demand followers as well as leaders. Sometimes we think that we are extremely independent and do not want to be led. Actually, we often are hoping for leaders to emerge. Even though we want to be involved in what is taking place, we do not inherently reject leadership. We want to follow as well as to participate in leading.

What Leadership Is

Our focus in this chapter is on the concept and practice of leadership. This is an issue that arises when we consider Matthew's story (Matt. 20:20-28). Our discussion below focuses on the types of leadership, definitions of leadership, factors to be considered in leadership, and my own definition of leadership.

First, there are several types of leaders, and many people can lead. Murray G. Ross and Charles E. Hendry distinguish three types of leaders:

> (1) the person who has achieved pre-eminence by unique attainment, who is *ahead* of his group, a person of the caliber of an Einstein; (2) the person who by designation, for whatever reason, has been given official leadership status involving formal authority, who is *the head* of his group; and (3) the person who emerges in a given situation as capable of helping the group determine and achieve its objectives and/or maintain and strengthen the group itself, who is *a head* of his group." (1957, 15, Italics mine)

To illustrate this, in Biblical terms we can think of the prophet, the priest, and the king. The prophet is usually *ahead* of his followers. He is a seer and has insight into where history is going. The priest is *a head* of his followers. He is one of the spiritual leaders who guides the people. The king is *the head* of his followers. The king has the full power and the position to rule the people of his group. Some kings are more considerate than others of the wishes of the people, but the king has the power.

In a supreme and unique sense, Christ is all three—Prophet, Priest, and King! According to Acts 7:37, God will raise up a prophet like Moses. That prophet is Jesus. The writer of Hebrews declares that we have a high priest "who has taken His seat at the right hand of the throne of the Majesty in the heavens" (Heb. 8:1). That high priest is Jesus. When Christ returns, He will have a name written on His robe and His thigh which will be "KING OF KINGS, AND LORD OF LORDS" (Rev. 19:16). That King is Jesus. Jesus Christ fulfils all three roles supremely.

Second, we want to know what leadership is. There are many definitions of leadership. John C. Maxwell states, "Everyone talks about it; few understand it. Most people want it; few achieve it. There are over fifty definitions and descriptions of it in my personal files" (1993, 1).

Even though there are many definitions of leadership, and leadership is difficult to define, we often know it when we see it. It is like the wind blowing—we see the result.

Many definitions focus on the last two types mentioned by Ross and Hendry, the leader who is either *the head* or *a head* of his group. Not as much attention is devoted to the leader who is *ahead* of his peers. Sometimes a person who is *ahead* of a group becomes *the head* or *a head*, but not always. Like a prophet, he may or may not be well accepted by the group. The definitions below focus mainly on *a head* or *the head*; but the one who is *ahead* of his peers is not excluded.

One. In Matthew's story, the mother of James and John asked Jesus to seat them on the right and left hands of Jesus (vv. 20-21). Apparently, they had in mind a temporal kingdom and political leadership. So I will mention several definitions of leadership from the political world.

Political leaders often put a strong emphasis on the position, power, and authority of the leader. Writing about the nature of political processes, Charles Hickman Titus states, "Leadership, synonymous with politics, is the art of getting what one wants and making people like it" (1950). President Truman's definition is similar. According to J. Oswald Sanders, he stated that "A leader is a person who has the ability to get others to do what they don't want to do, and like it" (1967, 19). These definitions do not focus on the needs, wants, and desires of the people being led. In these definitions, neither Titus nor Truman mentions service. They may elsewhere, but not here.

According to James L. Fisher, Eisenhower, who was both a military and political leader, defined leadership as follows: "Leadership is the art of getting someone else to do something you want done because he wants to do it" (1984, 15). This definition brings in the desires of the people being led. While still emphasizing the strong role of the leader and the ability to persuade, this definition comes closer than the other two toward identifying service as being an essential element in leadership. Many political leaders talk about service, but obtaining power is often, if not always, an important goal.

When you watch the political pundits on TV, they seem to be conflicted about the nature of leadership. They want political leaders to be responsive to the people they lead. However, they will criticize the leaders for following the polls. In addition, they often applaud the leaders for taking an unpopular stand and then persuading the people to follow. Or they may criticize the leaders for not "listening" to the people. So it is difficult to "win" with many of the pundits.

Two. Turning from political leadership to leadership in general, quite a few stress the idea that leadership is, or at least involves, influence and, for many, the self-fulfillment of the people being led. For example, Emory S. Bogardus says, "A *leader* is a person who exerts special influence over a number of people" (1934, 3). In addition, he states that "Leadership is a process in which there is a give-and-take between leader and followers. ... The leader must thus consider continually the various possible reactions of his followers" (1934, 6-7).

Similarly Ordway Tead states that "*Leadership is the activity of influencing people to cooperate toward some goal which they come to find desirable*" (1935, 20). He goes on to say "The unique emphasis in the idea of leading here advanced, is upon the satisfaction and sense of self-fulfillment secured by the followers of the true leader" (1935, 20). Both these definitions include the concept of influence and the relationship the leader has with the followers.

Three. Many authors write from a Christian perspective. They often acknowledge that many good leadership principles are not uniquely Christian, but they include them in their overall Christian framework. The idea of leadership as influence, as well as other factors, is widely accepted.

Maxwell, for example, defines leadership as follows: "After more than four decades of observing leadership within my family and many years of developing my own leadership potential, I have come to this conclusion: *Leadership is influence*. That's it. Nothing more; nothing less" (1993, 1). Similarly, James C. Hunter defines leadership as: "The *skills* of *influencing* people to enthusiastically work toward goals identified as being for the common good, with *character* that inspires confidence" (2004, 32).

Ken Blanchard and Phil Hodges posit that "Leadership is a process of influence. Anytime you seek to influence the thinking, behavior, or development of people toward accomplishing a goal in their personal or professional lives, you are taking on the role of a leader" (2005, 5). They advocate leading like Jesus. According to them, the leader is a servant, not a self-serving leader.

J. Robert Clinton holds that "A leader is a person with God-given capacity and God-given responsibility who influences a group of followers towards God's purposes for the group. The central element of this definition is the leader influencing the group toward God's purposes" (1988, 127). Similarly, Henry and Richard Blackaby maintain that "Spiritual leadership is moving people on to God's agenda" (2011, 36). In order to do this, they say spiritual leaders must hear from God. They maintain that "Spiritual leaders cannot know God's agenda if they are disoriented to his voice. As with any facet of the Christian life, it always comes down to one thing. The most important thing spiritual leaders do is cultivate their relationship with God (John 15:5; Jeremiah 7:13)" (2011, 42).

Third, as we think about various definitions of leadership, at least eight factors emerge for our consideration. In this section, I have commented on seven of these factors. The eighth factor is service. Because service is the main factor in Matthew's story, I have treated it in a separate section. The theories of leadership usually highlight one or more of these factors. A complete definition of leadership will encompass all of them.

One. Let us consider the leader himself. The leader is obviously an important factor. His background, personality, and traits are a part of the total leadership picture. Ross and Hendry say that the "great man" theory holds that men are predestined by their unusual natural traits to lead events and shape situations (1957, 18). Other theories emphasize the training and the development of leadership qualities.

Our Bible colleges and universities stress the training of leaders. It is commonly believed among us that most individuals will have stronger and more fruitful ministries if they are trained to serve. Nevertheless, we all recognize that God sometimes chooses someone to lead—whether pastor, evangelist, or teacher—in powerful and unusual ways who has not been trained in one of our institutions.

Two. As Richard Wolff points out, leadership may be seen as "a group property and as a function of the group structure. The significance of the leader is recognized, but largely because he is seen as the dynamic focus of the group" (1970, 113). The leader assists the group in achieving its goals, with its functions, and helps maintain the group.

Many churches are planted by an individual who is called of God for this task. However, there are other churches that are started by a group which looks for a pastor to become the leader. In such cases, the group has an important role in the planting of the church.

Three. Another approach emphasizes the situation. Leaders are involved in many different situations. It would not be wise nor practical for a given person to be a leader in every situation. Thus, a leader in one situation may not be a leader in another situation. Sometimes a leader in one situation is very much a follower in another situation. Moreover, the practices that produce a result in one situation may not work very well in another situation. A pastor might have a huge result in one city and then write the story with an emphasis on how this was done. Then the pastor goes to another city and does not see the same harvest.

According to Wolff, the leader, the group, and the situation are all important elements in leadership. After discussing the leader and the group, he makes this statement:

> Finally, it has been suggested that leadership is situational. It is argued that a leader may be ineffective in situations where his abilities are not useful. Since personality traits are stable or fixed, whereas group goals and purposes are variable, it has been deduced that leadership must be fluid and move from one member of the group to another, depending on the situation (1970, 113-114)

Wolff concludes that "We are then face to face with three basic concepts of leadership: the center of gravity is either in the leader, in the group, or in the situation" (1979, 114). My conclusion is that wherever we place the center of gravity, we can include all these factors in our definition of leadership.

Four. In any leadership situation, both private and group goals exist. As Christians, we submit ourselves to the will of God. Because of this, the challenge is to discover what His will is, both for us as individuals and for the group. Henry and Richard Blackaby stress that "Spiritual leaders work from God's agenda" (2011, 40). They maintain that "God is working throughout the world to achieve his purposes and to advance his kingdom. His concern is not to fulfil leaders' dreams and goals or to build their kingdoms and careers" (2011, 40).

Both the leader and the group must sense the leadership of the Holy Spirit. Leaders may focus on what the group initiates and wants, what the leaders want, or what the group comes to find desirable under their guidance. The important point is that they all hear from God. In church life, very often the lead pastor hears from God, shares the vision with other leaders in the church, and presents the vision to the congregation. When the congregation is united in believing in the vision, great things can be done.

Five. The act of leading is described in various terms. Some speak of the leader getting what he wants and making people like it. Others stress more what the leader does to influence or guide the group. Going further, others put the emphasis on the leader being mainly an implementer of group goals. Whatever approach is taken, the ideal is for the leader and the people to work and move together. A prophet, of course, is frequently found out front and alone. He walks where others do not wish to walk or, perhaps, fear to walk!

Six. A very important factor in leadership is vision. Although Maxwell defines leadership as influence, he expresses this opinion: "My observation over the last twenty years has been that all effective leaders have a vision of what they must accomplish" (1993, 139). With regard to the source of the vision, George Barna holds that "True vision comes from God. When we personally conjure up a vision, it is fallible, flawed, and limited; God's vision is perfect in every way" (1997, 48).

Seven. With regard to Christian leadership, the work of the Holy Spirit is the most important factor. Administration (1 Cor.12:28), for example, is a gift of the Spirit. In addition, the Spirit uses the natural talents that we have. Even these natural talents are themselves gifts from God. Moreover, the Spirit guides both the leader and the group toward the goals God sets before them.

Fourth, many years ago, with the above factors in mind, I wrote my own definition of leadership. With slight modifications, I will present this definition today. As you will see, it is somewhat eclectic and inclusive of the seven factors just discussed plus service. Here is my definition:

Leadership is the art, science, and gift of the Holy Spirit demonstrated by a person, in a given situation, by means of which a group and its constituency are inspired, guided, and served, in the cooperative accomplishment of a vision which is accepted by the group as the will of God and desirable, whether the objectives of the vision were formed by the group or presented to the group by the leader.

This definition is in total harmony with the emphasis on servant leadership by Jesus in Matthew's and Mark's story. The leader serves the ones whom he leads and the people they serve. With this in mind, we turn to a discussion of service as the indispensable element in spiritual leadership.

Service and Greatness

Many writers, both secular and Christian, hold that the great leader is one who puts service first, rather than power. This has led some of these writers to develop the concept of servant leadership. They show that leading by serving is an excellent way to lead. We can add that it should be a desired element in all approaches to leadership. Some approaches, however, preclude the idea of servant leadership.

As we consider greatness and leadership, it important to note that these are not totally synonymous terms. These terms overlap when many who are great become great through their leadership. However, there are great people who are not leaders, and there are leaders who are not great. Our focus here is on being great servant leaders.

First, according to some sources, Robert K. Greenleaf is the "father" of the concept of servant leadership in the secular world. He did not base his work on what Jesus said in the stories by Matthew and Mark. Rather, he chose a story by Hermann Hesse which had to do with a person named Leo who led by serving. In an essay that Greenleaf wrote in 1970, he introduced the term "servant leadership." Later in his book, he makes this descriptive statement:

The idea of the servant as leader came out of reading Hermann Hesse's *Journey to the East*. In this story we see a band of men on a mythical journey, probably also Hesse's own journey. The central figure of the story is Leo, who accompanies the part as the *servant* who does their menial chores, but who also sustains them with his spirit and his song. He is a person of extraordinary presence. All goes well until Leo disappears. Then the group falls into disarray and the journey is abandoned. They cannot make it without the servant Leo. The narrator, one of the party, after some years of wandering, finds Leo and is taken into the Order that has sponsored the journey. There he discovers that Leo, whom he had known first as servant, was in fact the titular head of the Order, its guiding spirit, a great and noble *leader*. (Greenleaf, 2002)

According to Greenleaf, "this story clearly says that *the great leader is seen as servant first*, and that simple fact is the key to his greatness" (2002). He applies this insight to many domains as he comments on servant leadership in business, education, churches, and foundations.

Second, almost 2000 years earlier, Matthew and Mark wrote the story of Jesus interacting with the disciples about service and leadership. This book deals with the leadership issues raised by that story. In the story, Jesus declared: "Whoever wishes to become great among you shall be your servant, and whoever wishes to be first among you shall be your slave" (Matt. 20:26-27). Without service, one does not become a great leader. In other words, the indispensable element in greatness and in great leadership is service. Moreover, to be first among others, one must step down and be a slave.

When authors, both secular and Christian, write about servant leadership, they often cite this story. It is, indeed, a powerful story that inverts the normal values of a secular society. Individual believers in Christ, as well as the church, need to act in accordance with what Jesus taught and did. Many secular businesses and institutions have captured the essence of what Jesus taught and used His teaching in productive ways.

Service, then, is the indispensable factor in greatness and, we may add, of servant leadership. Jesus contrasted this with the "Gentile" concept of greatness and their view of leadership. For the Gentiles, greatness and leadership did not exist without power. Without power, all was lost. Jesus exhorted the disciples to make service the indispensable element of greatness and leadership. Without service, the disciples do not lead. All the power in the world would not make them leaders in the sense that Christ spoke of leadership.

Conclusion

The story by Matthew about the mother of James and John asking that her sons have positions of honor in Christ's kingdom raises many issues about leadership. In this chapter, we have focused on what leadership is.

First, I have discussed the need for leaders. We have been given an enormous task in evangelism, discipleship, training, and compassion ministries, and there is a demand for leaders. Second, I included a section on what leadership is. This identified the types of leadership, definitions of leadership, seven major factors in leadership, and my definition of leadership. Third, I presented a discussion of service and greatness, including both a secular approach and the story by Matthew and Mark.

As we conclude this chapter, let us simply exalt Jesus. In His leadership, as in all other things, He is our highest example. When we look at Jesus, we are inspired to follow His example and accomplish His task in His way. His emphasis in the Matthew and Mark story is on becoming great through service. As we do our work, we need to focus on serving the people we seek to reach.

CHAPTER TWO

THE DESIRE TO LEAD

Introduction

When our two sons were young boys, one of them asked me, "Dad, is it right to want to be the greatest preacher in the world?" As I recall, I did not have a very good answer at the time. He had asked a very profound question, one which still challenges me to think very deeply. To some degree, I believe we are all challenged by this question.

Our subject in this chapter is "The Desire to Lead." As previously stated, we are basing this book on the story in Matthew 20:20-28. This story raises many leadership issues. We will read again the entire story, but we will focus our attention in this chapter on verses 20-21. In these two verses, the issue of the desire to lead arises.

[20] Then the mother of the sons of Zebedee came to Jesus with her sons, bowing down and making a request of Him.

[21] And He said to her, "What do you wish?"

She said to Him, "Command that in Your kingdom these two sons of mine may sit one on Your right and one on Your left."

[22] But Jesus answered, "You do not know what you are asking. Are you able to drink the cup that I am about to drink?" They said to Him, "We are able."

[23] He said to them, "My cup you shall drink; but to sit on My right and on *My* left, this is not Mine to give, but it is for those for whom it has been prepared by My Father."

[24] And hearing *this*, the ten became indignant with the two brothers.

[25] But Jesus called them to Himself and said, "You know that the rulers of the Gentiles lord it over them, and *their* great men exercise authority over them.

[26] It is not this way among you, but whoever wishes to become great among you shall be your servant.

[27] and whoever wishes to be first among you shall be your slave;

[28] just as the Son of Man did not come to be served, but to serve, and to give His life a ransom for many."

Our feelings about whether or not we should want to be leaders are often very mixed. Our Bible schools are built with leadership training in mind. The same is true of local church training programs. Nevertheless, we sometimes make students feel guilty when they want to lead.

When I have asked students whether or not they want to be leaders, I have received mixed replies. Some have replied, "Yes" or "No" without any qualifying comments. Others have qualified their answers with statements such as, "It depends on what you mean by leader." Some replied "Yes, in God's sight," or "No, not in man's eyes." If I were to suggest that a qualified answer would suffice, I believe most would give such a response. What I mean by "leader" in my question is important to their replies.

Several points attract our attention as we consider the desire to lead. We will discuss (1) the desired positions, (2) the reply of Jesus, (3) our evaluation of the desire to lead, and (4) the results of leadership through service. All these points will help us with our feelings about wanting to lead.

The Desired Positions

First, Mark indicates that James and John came to Jesus with the request to sit on His left and right hands in His kingdom. However, Matthew says their mother came with James and John and made the request. Obviously, all three were in agreement. Concerning this point, Frank Stagg presents this view: "Whether Matthew is removing some of the blame from the two disciples or simply supplying further detail to Mark's account, both Matthew and Mark show that the disciples themselves were responsible for the selfish and benighted request" (1969, 195).

Second, the mother of James and John is generally thought to be Salome (Matt. 27:55-56; Mark 15:40; 16:1; John 19:25). Whether Salome or Mary, the wife of Clopas, was the sister of Mary, the mother of Jesus, is sometimes debated. If Salome was the sister of Mary, the mother of Jesus, she was the aunt of Jesus. Whatever conclusion is reached about this, with the support of James and John, Salome's request (verse 21), was, "Command that in Your kingdom these two sons of mine may sit one on Your right and one on Your left."

Third, many commentators make the point that the disciples, including James, John, and their mother were expecting a temporal Kingdom on earth. Others maintain that the kingdom they expected was like the future Jewish messianic Kingdom. Concerning a temporal Kingdom, Albert Barnes proposes that:

> They were still looking for a temporal kingdom. They expected that he would reign on the earth with great pomp and glory. They anticipated that he would conquer as a prince and a warrior. They wished to be distinguished in the day of his triumph. . . . The disciples, here, had no reference to the kingdom of heaven, but only to the kingdom which they supposed he was about to set upon the earth." (1987 Reprint, 208)

According to James D. Smart, James and John had in mind the Jewish conception of a future Kingdom. The future Kingdom would be both temporal and unending. He holds that:

> James and John share with the others, as becomes plain in verse 41 [Mark 10:41], the current Jewish conception of a future world order in which the nations, in being subjected to God's law, would be subjected to a perfected Israel and the whole world would be ruled from Jerusalem. What James and John are asking is not places of precedence in an enlarged disciple group or in a future church but places of the highest responsibility in a future world kingdom as Jesus' first assistants. (1979, 290)

The text does not actually say what the kingdom was that the disciples expected. However, it seems clear that there was a gap in understanding between what Jesus taught and what the disciples understood. We see this gap even as late as between His resurrection and His ascension when Jesus interacted with the disciples as follows (Acts 1:6-8):

> [6]So when they had come together, they were asking Him, saying, "Lord, is it at this time You are restoring the kingdom to Israel?"
> [7]He said to them, "It is not for you to know times or epochs which the Father has fixed by His own authority;
> [8]but you will receive power when the Holy Spirit has come upon you; and you shall be My witnesses both in Jerusalem, and in all Judea and Samaria, and even to the remotest part of the earth."

Fourth, the evaluation of scholars concerning Salome and her request range from condemnation to what I would call conditional approval. As John C. Hutchinson indicates, Jesus had already promised that the disciples would rule (Matt. 19:28) in His messianic Kingdom (2009, 57). The request of the disciples had to do with prominence in the Kingdom. Given the understanding the disciples had concerning Christ's kingdom and other factors, some scholars are reluctant to condemn their mother or the disciples for making this request. William Hendriksen, who accepts the view that Salome was the aunt of Jesus, does not condemn her. He makes these comments:

> Besides, if our assumption that she was probably Jesus' aunt should be correct, this family relationship may also have encouraged her to make her request. But even if this should not be correct, at least she knew very well that within the largest circle of Christ's followers there was another, smaller circle, namely, The Twelve; that concentric with these two, but still smaller, was the circle of The Three; and finally, that two of these three were her own sons, James and John. Now, then, if the reign of God in all its splendor should be established next month or perhaps even next week, and Jesus should be enthroned in majesty, should not her sons be seated at his right and left? Was not this the way of kings and other dignitaries? See Exod. 17:12; II Sam. 16:6; I Kings 22:19; (II Chron. 18:18); Neh. 8:4. (1973, 747-748)

Mothers will do things like this! Many years ago, my father and mother were serving as missionaries in Senegal. They were invited by the American Embassy in Dakar, Senegal, to a reception for Vice-President Lyndon Johnson and his wife, Lady Bird. They were in the greeting line when Mom decided to ask the Vice-President to write to her sons, my brother and me. When she was shaking hands with the Johnsons, she made her request. Lady Bird wrote a note about this and put it in her purse. Sometime later we received a letter, signed by the Vice-President, in which he said the following:

Dear "Flatterys,"

When Lady Bird and I got back from Dakar and she cleaned out her pocketbook, she found a note she had made during our visit. We met your parents in Dakar at a reception given at the American Embassy and promised we would write you. They looked well and seemed to be enjoying their work in Senegal. It was nice to meet some fellow Texans in that faraway place.

Mom and Dad were not Texans, but my wife, Esther, and I were living in Texas at the time.

The request of Salome, along with James and John, was a far more serious matter, but the actions of a mother on behalf of her sons are well understood by us. As a result, many tend not to be severe in their judgment. Matthew does not tell us exactly what their full motivation was, but it appears to me that it was mixed. They were motivated to follow Jesus, but mixed in a very human desire for position and honor.

Fifth, we can draw upon the Old Testament to understand Salome's request. The stories of Bathsheba and Ezra illustrate the importance of being seated on the right hand and left hand of a person in leadership.

One. Adonijah, the brother of Solomon, went to Bathsheba and persuaded her to ask Solomon to give him Abishag the Shunammite as a wife. When Bathsheba went to her son Solomon, the king arose to meet her, bowed before her, and sat on his throne (1 Kings 2:19). Then, he had a throne set for her, and she sat on his right. Sitting at the king's right was clearly a place of high honor.

At this point, Bathsheba made her request. Although she was sitting in a place of honor, her request was not granted. Solomon correctly assessed the situation, blamed Adonijah for the request, and had him executed. He told his mother that she might as well have asked him to give the kingdom to Adonijah.

Two. Ezra the scribe was called upon to read the law of Moses to the people (Neh. 8:1-4). They had gathered at the square which was in front of the Water Gate. Ezra stood at a wooden podium which was made for this purpose. He was accompanied on each side by a group of men. These assistants stood at his right hand and at his left. The presence of these men at his right hand and left hand suggests honor, delegated power, and responsibility.

Being at the right and left hands of a leader in Old Testament times suggested honor, power, and position. This was not only a common meaning in the Old Testament, but it has been in many cultures throughout history. In a royal court, both the right hand and the left hands are places of honor. The left hand is only slightly less glorious than the right.

Sixth, Salome may have understood that her sons would be called upon to serve others, but she wanted them to have positions of honor, power, and fame. The common meaning of "right hand" and "left hand," the indignation of the disciples, and the reply by Jesus all suggest this. She wanted her sons to be prominent in the kingdom.

With regard to Salome's request, R. C. H. Lenski posits that, "Despite all its fault, Salome's request contains something worth noting. All about us men seek the world's honor and high places; here are three persons who put the βασιλεία [kingdom] and δόξα [glory] of Christ above everything else. The wish of Salome, duly purified, has been seconded by many a mother who prayed for her son that he might serve Christ is some high work in his church" (1943, 786-787).

The Reply of Jesus

Jesus did not condemn Salome, James, or John for their desire to lead. Rather, he responded by showing them the cost of true leadership and by defining leadership for them. Rather than condemning them for their desire to lead, He showed them the way. His explanation begins with the price of leadership.

First, Jesus confronted the disciples with the price of leadership. He asked, "Are you able to drink the cup that I am about to drink?" On this point, Lenski cites Luther and Augustine. According to Luther, the ambition of these disciples springs from faith and needs only to be purified. Augustine said, "They sought the exaltation but did not see the step" (1943, 787). The "step" usually shortens the line of "would be" leaders. Real leadership, as Jesus would define it, usually has a high cost. I will discuss the price of leadership more fully in our next chapter.

Second, Jesus defined greatness. A good definition identifies what a thing is and what it is not. Jesus said what true greatness is not. It does not make power the indispensable element. People can be great without being in positions of power. Jesus said also what the essence of true greatness is. The indispensable factor of greatness is service. Those who would be great must be the servant of all. Without this, they are not great.

Third, Jesus recognizes without condemnation that some have the will to be great. When people have the desire and determination to be great in service, much good can be done. We must remember, however, that servanthood is itself a position with its own greatness. Other positions may come to the servant, but he must be willing to serve without them.

Fourth, the reply of Jesus is paradoxical. True leadership puts service before power and honor. By putting service first, one can become a true leader. By putting power and honor first, one loses true leadership. This is true not only of leadership in the Kingdom of God but in secular contexts as well. Writers such as Greenleaf have stressed servant leadership both in the church and in secular environments.

Jesus does not condemn the desire to lead. He redirects that desire from position and power to service. Sanders observes that "an ambition which has as its center the glory of God and the welfare of His church is not only legitimate but positively praiseworthy" (1967, 11). Similarly, Wolff states, "Legitimate ambition, the desire to be a leader, does not run counter to true humility. Paul's admonition, 'In humility count others better than yourselves' (Phil. 2:3), does not abolish the concept of leadership" (1970, 13). The desire to lead, when kept in its proper perspective, is not condemned. Jesus captures this motivational force, puts it in proper perspective, redirects it, and uses it for very productive purposes. This gives us a wholesome approach toward the desire to lead and helps us to proceed without ambivalence.

Evaluation

The desire to lead can be right. Paul wrote in 1 Timothy 3:1, "To aspire to leadership is an honorable ambition" (NEB). The NASB has this translation: "It is a trustworthy statement: if any man aspires to the office of overseer, it is a fine work he desires *to do*."

First, here Paul clearly approves of the desire to lead. He sees the office of overseer as an opportunity for someone to serve. Thus, he does not put down the desire for this office. Instead, he puts his blessing on it.

In church circles, we tend to not be very open about the desire to lead. For example, anyone who lets on that he or she wants to be the General Superintendent would likely be ruled out. However, we all know that some ministers have that desire. The lack of openness is not true in all cultures.

On one occasion, as president of ICI (now Global University), I flew into the Philippines to conduct business for our school. I was met by a minister who said, "I would like to be the General Superintendent, but if I do not get elected, I would like to be the pastor of Bethel Temple. And if I do not get elected as pastor, I would be willing to be the ICI director." Whether that was just his approach or a culturally accepted way, I do not know; but it clearly showed us how we ranked in his mind. In our country, few in the church would take this approach.

Whether or not we approve of the desire to lead depends to some degree on our culture and values. Please observe the following categories. In our culture, we would consider the desire to be a pastor as good and one that we can admit, but we are more ambivalent about the desire to be a presbyter or superintendent. Even though the desire might be considered honorable, few would admit to having it. Some motives are not considered the best, such as wanting a luxury car, but we are willing to admit it. Other motives, such as personal aggrandizement, are considered bad, and we do not readily admit them.

Second, to desire to lead through service is both honorable and important. We should not be ambivalent about this. Some people have become leaders when initially they did not want to lead. However, as they acquiesce to the will of God, the desire to lead is to some extent born. Others begin with a greater desire to lead.

Sanders illustrates the issue of the desire to lead from the life of William E. Sangster. In a private manuscript found after his death, Sangster records his growing conviction that he should be a leader in the Methodist church. Sangster wrote:

- This is the will of God for me. I did not choose it. I sought to escape it. But it has come.
- Something else has come too. A sense of certainty that God does not want me only for a preacher. He wants me also for a leader—a leader in Methodism.
- I feel a commissioning to work under God for the revival of this branch of His Church—careless of my own reputation; indifferent to the comments of older and jealous men.
- I am thirty-six. If I am to serve God in this way, I must no longer shrink from the task—but do it.
- I have examined my heart for ambition. I am certain it is not there. I hate the criticism I shall evoke and the painful chatter of people. Obscurity, quiet browsing among books, and the service of simple people is my taste—but by the will of God, this is my task. God help me.

- Bewildered and unbelieving, I hear the voice of God say to me: "I want to sound the note through you." O God, did ever an apostle shrink from his task more? I dare not say "No" but, like Jonah, I would fain run away. (1967, 22, bullets mine, from Doctor Sangster, by Paul Sangster, 109)

In this story, one can sense the ambivalence of a would-be leader. In the end, he accepted that it was God's will for him to be a leader in Methodism. Many church leaders seem to accept their role of leadership without going through a time of having this ambivalence. Ross and Hendry make this point:

The leader who has no desire to be the leader is often a person who is ambivalent, if not disinterested, in his leadership role. It has been suggested that persons with insistent needs for dominance, power, and prestige may be expected to have higher potentialities for leadership. This may be, but certainly it can be said that only those with some desire for leadership will be sufficiently motivated to undertake the responsibilities implicit in leadership and thus satisfy the needs of their followers, who, as we will see, desire as leader someone with initiative, a sense of responsibility, and willingness to serve the group interests. (1943, 54-55)

Third, the desire to lead can, obviously, be wrong. We must guard against this at all costs. As Jesus proclaims, some people desire to be great; and others, going further, desire to be first. Wanting to be first is a more intense desire to lead. Some people have an extreme desire to lead with too much emphasis on power.

We can recognize the symptoms of such an extreme desire in the lives of some would-be leaders. Very often, they emphasize expediency over principle. For them, the end justifies the means. We often see great selfishness and the raw exercise of power in reaching various objectives. Generally, such people disdain others and will step on others to get to the top.

Such people existed in New Testament times as well as ours. John states, "I wrote something to the church; but Diotrephes, who loves to be first among them, does not accept what we say" (3 John 9). As the KJV puts it, Diotrephes loved to have the "preeminence." Clearly, John was unhappy with his attitude.

Fourth, as believers, we can consider as dead the motives which are by nature wrong. Also, we can subdue motives that have become wrong because we have allowed them to become predominant. The Holy Spirit will help us do these things.

Even so, our motives, at best, are somewhat mixed. We often speak as though we can be solely and purely motivated by love and service. Thank God, with the help of the Holy Spirit, these motives can dominate our lives. However, we usually also are motivated to some extent by what we might call "enlightened self-interest." Kept in proper perspective, this is not wrong. Citing the law in Leviticus 19:18, Jesus said, "You shall love your neighbor as yourself" (Matt. 22:39).

With regard to great leadership, the indispensable feature is service. As long as men desire to serve and keep other legitimate motives secondary, they remain true to their Christian beliefs. Other motives can be captured, disciplined, and put to use for the glory of God.

Fifth, especially in Christian leadership, but also in other contexts, the pathway to leadership is paradoxical. R. Earl Allen puts this squarely in focus with this comment: "Men pray for God to humble them and at the same time attempt to exalt themselves. We are to humble ourselves and let God do the exalting" (1963, 117). We see the paradox of the way to exaltation in Peter's advice to the saints concerning humility and exaltation (1 Pet. 5:5-6).

> ⁵You younger men, likewise, be subject to *your* elders; and all of you, clothe yourselves with humility toward one another, for GOD IS OPPOSED TO THE PROUD, BUT GIVES GRACE TO THE HUMBLE.
> ⁶Therefore humble yourselves under the mighty hand of God, that He may exalt you at the proper time.

Humility may or may not lead to a position in the kingdom, but God will certainly reward us at the right time and in the right way. A sure way to be ruled out of Christian leadership, however, is to approach it through pride and self-exaltation. Peter wisely advises us to be humble. Paradoxically, it often opens the door to important leadership roles.

Results of Leadership through Service

Salome wanted her two sons to have places of prominence in the kingdom. Without rebuking James and John, Jesus encouraged them and the other disciples to lead through service. When we follow this path, what will be the results for us?

First, the man who wants to lead through service will have ample opportunity to serve. He will be able, no doubt, to meet many needs and help others. This does not mean, however, that he will have a place of prominence, position, and power in this life. He may well serve all his life without a leadership position.

Second, sometimes, a person renders great service without any recognition. Even the service itself goes unnoticed. When a person continues to serve under such circumstances, his true greatness is only enhanced. Sooner or later, most of us are tested on this very point. Once again, we can take comfort that a just and loving God will reward us appropriately. We know that God will appropriately honor us, whether in this life or the life to come.

Third, many times people are honored for their service. The service itself is recognized. Moreover, those who serve sometimes come into places of honor and power. Thus, they become great in both the eyes of God and men. Such people, however, will lose the approval of God unless they continue to lead through service. Service is the indispensable aspect of leadership.

Conclusion

We began with a question asked by one of our two sons, "Dad, is it right to want to be the greatest preacher in the world?" If one of your sons or daughters asked you this question, how would you answer? At this point, I would say, "Yes, providing you lead through service and put service ahead of all other motives. Then, whether you are recognized or not, you will not be disappointed."

The times, human conditions, and the commands of Christ all demand that we lead. We cannot accomplish all that we must do without leaders and leadership. We must not be ambivalent about this. Rather, we need to properly define leadership, commit ourselves to paying the price, and take up the task of leading through service. May God give us many leaders!

CHAPTER THREE
THE PRICE OF LEADERSHIP
Introduction

When ICI University was located in Irving, Texas, we had many guests. I would occasionally take some of them to see the place where President John F. Kennedy was shot and the memorial to him on the sixth floor of the old Texas School Book Depository building in Dallas, Texas. One of the pictures on the sixth floor is of the presidential motorcade passing the Adolphus Hotel on Main Street. If the picture were clearer, I would be seen in it because I was standing there when the motorcade went by.

In 1963, my wife, Esther, our two sons, George and Mark, and I were living in Richardson, Texas, just north of Dallas. We were planting a new church in that community. About noon on November 22, 1963, I drove from Oak Cliff into the heart of Dallas and parked my car in the Adolphus Hotel parking garage. I walked outside to stand on Main Street to watch the presidential motorcade.

There was a huge crowd with many people surging into the street to be near the passing motorcycles, limousines, and cars. Eventually, the presidential car came into view and passed by with President Kennedy, his wife Jackie, and Governor Connally in the car. I almost could have touched the car as it went by. I was standing just a few blocks away from where President Kennedy was shot.

The shooting occurred too far away for me to hear any gunfire or see anything. When the motorcade passed, I returned to my car and drove up Central Expressway. I turned on my radio and heard the words, "The President has been shot." I drove on to Richardson, entered my home, and began praying about what I would say to our congregation. It was then that I began thinking about the enormous price there is to leadership. President Kennedy paid the ultimate price.

This incident brings me to my subject and my text for this chapter. My subject is "The Price of Leadership." My text for this book is Matthew 20:20-28; for this chapter it is verse 22. In this verse, Jesus challenges the disciples with a question about paying the cost of leading. Matthew 20:20-28 tells the story:

> ²⁰Then the mother of the sons of Zebedee came to Jesus with her sons, bowing down and making a request of Him.
> ²¹And He said to her, "What do you wish?"
> She said to Him, "Command that in Your kingdom these two sons of mine may sit one on Your right and one on Your left."
> ²²But Jesus answered, "You do not know what you are asking. Are you able to drink the cup that I am about to drink?" They said to Him, "We are able."
> ²³He said to them, "My cup you shall drink; but to sit on My right and on *My* left, this is not Mine to give, but it is for those for whom it has been prepared by My Father."
> ²⁴And hearing *this*, the ten became indignant with the two brothers.
> ²⁵But Jesus called them to Himself and said, "You know that the rulers of the Gentiles lord it over them, and *their* great men exercise authority over them.
> ²⁶It is not this way among you, but whoever wishes to become great among you shall be your servant.
> ²⁷and whoever wishes to be first among you shall be your slave;
> ²⁸just as the Son of Man did not come to be served, but to serve, and to give His life a ransom for many."

As we consider verse 22 and our subject, "The Price of Leadership," we will discuss (1) Christ's reply to the request of James and John and their mother, (2) some of the costs of leadership, and (3) meeting the challenge of leading.

Before we pick up these themes, however, let us briefly review and summarize some thoughts on leadership which we have thus far considered. There are at least three types of leaders. A leader can be *ahead, the head,* or *a head.* When we think of leaders, we often think of the last two types. However, all three types of leaders can influence others.

With this in mind, several points should be made: (1) Leadership may involve position, power, and authority. All these factors may be involved in what one does as a leader, but they may not be either. (2) The indispensable element of greatness in leadership is service. One may serve and be great with or without the other elements, such as power, being involved. (3) One may serve without leading in the sense of being *the head* or *a head*. (4) Sometimes one is a leader in the sense of being *ahead* in service.

Christ's Reply

The mother of James and John, the sons of Zebedee, came to Jesus and requested (verse 21), "Command that in Your kingdom these two sons of mine may sit one on Your right and one on Your left." Jesus' reply emphasized the price of leadership. True leadership may or may not involve position and honor, but it always exacts a price. We will now focus on Christ's reply.

First, Jesus responded, "You do not know what you are asking." The mother of James and John did not know all that her request would involve. She saw and wanted her sons to have the places of honor, but she did not see the cost. If she had seen the cost, she no doubt would have been more hesitant to make her request. Indeed, she may not have made the request at all.

Many budding leaders are unaware of the cost. Projects often involve more than they think it will. Sometimes, it may be better that we do not know the cost. When we started ICI (now Global University), we did not know how difficult it would be to produce high quality materials. It took years to develop what we projected in one committee meeting! I have met many people since who did not understand all that was involved. We could say the same thing about any place of leadership. We may try to count all the cost, but because of our ignorance, our estimate will fall short of the reality.

Jesus immediately touched on the crucial point—we should think of the cost before we offer ourselves for leadership. The leadership queue is much shorter when the cost is understood! By beginning here, Jesus did not have to condemn the disciples for their zealousness to lead.

Second, Jesus then asked, "Are you able to drink the cup that I am about to drink?" We will consider the cup He was about to drink, but before we do, let us examine the text. In the King James Version of Matthew 20:22-23, we read:

> [22]But Jesus answered and said, "Ye know not what ye ask. Are ye able to drink of the cup that I shall drink of, and to be baptized with the baptism that I am baptized with?" They say unto him, "We are able."

[23] And he saith unto them, "Ye shall drink indeed of my cup, and be baptized with the baptism that I am baptized with: but to sit on my right hand, and on my left, is not mine to give, but it shall be given to them for whom it is prepared of my Father." (KJV)

According to this version, Jesus refers both to the cup He would drink and the baptism He would experience. His reference to the baptism is not in the Nestle Greek version of the Matthew text. Also, the New American Standard Bible does not include the baptismal reference here.

However, the Nestle Greek text and the New American Standard Bible include the reference to baptism in the parallel passage in Mark 10:38-39. Here, in the NASB, we read:

[38] But Jesus said to them, "You do not know what you are asking. Are you able to drink the cup that I drink, or to be baptized with the baptism with which I am baptized?"

[39] They said to Him, "We are able." And Jesus said to them, "The cup that I drink you shall drink; and you shall be baptized with the baptism with which I am baptized."

Given the textual evidence in Mark, I believe that Jesus referred both to the cup He would drink and to the baptism He would experience. Both of the metaphors, the "cup" and the "baptism," depicted His suffering. To "drink" and to be "baptized" meant to endure the sufferings.

Third, Jesus suffered much in His earthly life and ministry. He gave up heaven's glories to become a man and dwell among us. He ministered in power and served others in dynamic ways. Yet He was rejected of men and despised. The sufferings He endured culminated in his passion (Latin *passio* means suffering) and death. The following points are germane.

One. When Jesus was in the Garden of Gethsemane, He prayed (Matt. 26:39), "My Father, if it is possible, let this cup pass from Me; yet not as I will, but as You will." Then, a second time, He prayed "My Father, if this cannot pass away unless I drink it, Your will be done" (Matt. 26:42). Jesus had to drink the "cup" in the Garden. The contents of this cup were the sins of men and the judgment of God.

With regard to our sins, Paul wrote (2 Cor. 5:21): "He made Him who knew no sin *to be* sin on our behalf, so that we might become the righteousness of God in Him." Few have written so eloquently on this point as Robert W. Cummings, one of my former teachers. On Gethsemane, he writes: "It is not the human weakness of Jesus that we see in Gethsemane; it is the recoil, the revulsion of the nature of the holy Son of God, when the One who was the sharer of God's holiness became sin, so that we might become righteousness" (1944, 34).

Concerning God's judgment, Christ is the One who paid the price of turning away God's anger and the covering for our sins. John states: "He is the atoning sacrifice for our sins, and not only for ours but also for the sins of the whole world" (1 John 2:2, NIV). The phrase "atoning sacrifice" is the NIV's translation of the Greek word *hilasmos* (*ἱλασμός*). The NASB translation is "propitiation" whereas the RSV has "expiation." According to Leon Morris, "Propitiation means the turning away of anger; expiation is rather the making amends for a wrong" (1983, 151). According to Burge, "The NIV attempts to catch both emphases with its translation, 'atoning sacrifice'" (1996, 86).

Putting all this in other words, the translation "atoning sacrifice" includes two concepts. Because of the price Jesus paid in the atonement, (1) God's anger is turned away from the one who believes in Jesus, and (2) the sins of the believer are wiped away and covered. All of this takes place because Jesus atoned for our sins.

The hymn "Jesus Paid It All" was written by Elvina Hall in 1865. She was a member of the Monument Street Methodist church. The hymn explicitly captures the essence of the second concept above, and no doubt presupposes the first. The lyrics include the following refrain:

> *Jesus paid it all*
> *All to Him I owe*
> *Sin had left a crimson stain*
> *He washed it white as snow*

Two. Jesus used the metaphor of baptism as well to describe His coming sufferings. The metaphors of the cup and of baptism give us a graphic portrayal of the suffering Jesus would endure. In Luke 12:49-50, Jesus declared:

> [49]"I have come to cast fire upon the earth; and how I wish it were already kindled!
>
> [50]But I have a baptism to undergo, and how distressed I am until it is accomplished."

The metaphor of baptism might refer to sufferings in general, but here Jesus especially refers to His death on the cross, to His work of atonement for our sins. In spite of the incredible suffering He would endure, Christ plainly says that He is eager to accomplish His atoning work.

Fourth, Jesus made it clear that His disciples would pay a price for following Him and for leading. He said (verse 23), "My cup you shall drink." The suffering of Jesus was unique in the sense that only He could take upon Himself our sins and atone for them, but the disciples, too, will suffer. For example, during the Passion Week, Jesus said, "Remember the word that I said to you, 'A slave is not greater than his master.' If they persecuted Me, they will also persecute you; if they kept My word, they will keep yours also" (John 15:20). When the way of the cross is difficult, we should be neither surprised nor dismayed. While we must be prepared for persecution, it is encouraging to know that there will be people who keep the word of Christ and who keep our word. Our word is our proclamation of the Word of Christ.

Your Cup and Baptism

As Christ has made clear, we will encounter sufferings along the trail to greatness in His kingdom. We will have our "cup" to drink and our "baptism" to undergo. We are applying this truth to leadership. We cannot be great leaders without paying the price of leadership. The persecution that Christ foretold is, of course, only one kind of price that leaders and disciples pay. Leaders are confronted with many different costs. Most, if not all, leaders have experienced one or more of these costs.

First, John W. Alexander avers that, "A penalty for leadership is loneliness" (1972, 110). The higher the position, the more lonely it is. There are fewer peers with whom to confide. Many leaders have found themselves entirely alone when they were confronted with difficult decisions. When the advisers have said everything, the decision still has to be made.

31

Second, because of their insight and understanding, leaders sometimes are ahead of their times. Seeing much, they want to effect change, to create, and to innovate. However, they often feel the pull of tradition and the slowness of others to accept change. In such situations, leaders must either slow down and wait for others to catch up or take the risk of forging ahead. Either way, the leader pays a price. The burden is easier to bear when the leader keeps his focus not only on what exists at the time, but also on the vision.

Third, many times leaders are misunderstood. Others may not understand their thinking or their motives. Rather paradoxically, a highly idealistic person is sometimes more misunderstood than others. Idealism forces openness and honesty, and openness and honesty reveal flaws. Sometimes leaders are misunderstood because they act on the basis of confidential information. People who do not have this information sometimes do not like the leader's decisions.

Fourth, Sanders writes, "No leader is exempt from criticism, and his humility will nowhere be seen more clearly than in the manner in which he accepts and reacts to it" (1967, 110). Perhaps this is the greatest test of all for leaders. Leaders must be able to endure and benefit from criticism.

Fifth, Fisher wrote a book about University presidents called *The Power of the President.* In it he emphasizes the positional distance that the University president must maintain. He explains his point of view as follows:

> Distance means being utterly transparent but always remote. Distance is having a close vice-presidential associate after ten years say, "Yes, he's my best friend and I would do virtually anything for him, but I can't say that I completely know him." Distance is recognizing that a leader is no longer "one of the boys or girls." Distance is being a friendly phantom: warm and genuine, concerned and interested, but rarely around too long or overly involved. Distance is recognizing and using the trappings of office, adjusting these only to suit the taste and sophistication of the audience or constituency. Distance balances remoteness and familiarity. The effective leader is both excitingly mysterious and utterly known. (1984, 45)

Many would-be leaders do not understand this concept nor can they live with the thought of being "distant" from followers. Yet positional distance appears to be an element in many leadership roles. It is a price that may be paid by those who would lead. As servant leaders in the body of Christ, we must be careful not to overdo this principle. People we serve like to feel that they know their leaders well.

Sixth, another cost is the loss of privacy. For many people this is a sacrifice. Somewhat paradoxically, people work to be leaders, then they bemoan the loss of privacy! Nevertheless, the loss can be real. Some leaders try to offset this by having unlisted phone numbers and by isolating themselves in other ways. Sometimes, however, the loss must be suffered in order to be close to the people being led.

Seventh, leaders must learn not only to lead but also to be subordinate. One cannot lead well unless he has learned to be subordinate also. It is interesting to watch leaders in various situations. A leader in one context strides confidently to the head place at the conference table; while in another situation, he quietly sits down in a subordinate place. The leader knows what his role is at all times.

Eighth, progress involves risk. He who will not take risks will not lead. The problem for Christian leaders is to know when action is born of faith and not presumption. We must listen carefully to people who issue words of caution, yet be ready to act when God fills our hearts with faith. Theodore Roosevelt famously said, "No man is worth his salt who is not ready at all times to risk his body, to risk his well-being, to risk his life, in a great cause" (thinkexist.com).

Ninth, most leaders invest more time and energy than their followers in the mission they seek to accomplish. Because of this, leaders can become very weary. Unless they are willing to pay this price, they probably will not be able to lead as well. This is particularly true when many volunteer leaders are involved. The leader has to lead by example.

At the same time, leaders must learn to delegate tasks to others and take opportunities to rest. When leaders are physically rested, they are more effective. Because leaders both need rest and, at the same time, have to sacrifice themselves in service, they live with tension that is probably never completely resolved.

Tenth, unfortunately, the leader's family often has to pay a price along with him or her. How many pastors have wished that they had taken more time with their children? When children go astray, they are especially prone to look back and wish they had done things differently. The leader must be careful to protect his family from paying too high a price.

Eleventh, often a group does not recognize a leader until he or she is gone. This especially is true of prophetic leaders. Such leaders often strike the consciences of those around them and see into the future with greater insight. Consequently, they are not accepted. However, all leaders are subject to rejection. As time goes on, they have to make unpopular decisions and take difficult courses of action. This eventually can result in rejection. This is a great price to pay.

Twelfth, Maxwell holds that the "price-tag" of leadership is self-discipline. He explains: "All great leaders have understood that their number one responsibility was for their own discipline and personal growth. If they could not lead themselves, they could not lead others. Leaders can never take others farther than they have gone themselves, for no one can travel without until he or she has first travelled within" (1993, 161-162).

We can lengthen the list. Leaders must pay the price of delayed reward: acceptable compromise in some cases, isolation, pressure and perplexity, never being off duty, disappointment, non-acceptance of vision, and many more. You can make your own list of costs you have paid.

Meeting the Challenge

Given the costs involved in leadership, we do not wonder now why Jesus did not rebuke the disciples for their mother's request. Instead, He pointed them to the price of leading. If we are to be leaders, we must be willing to pay the price.

We must meet the challenge. The writer of Proverbs 24:10 says, "If you are slack in the day of distress, Your strength is limited." In the KJV version of this verse, we read, "If you faint in the day of adversity, thy strength is small." Let us, then, consider how we can meet the challenge. With regard to meeting the challenge, I would note the following aspects.

First, when John F. Kennedy was shot, I thought a lot about the price of leadership. About five years later, in 1968, I was in Fort Worth in the home of Fred Scheuerman, my brother-in-law. At the time, Bobby Kennedy was in California campaigning for the Democratic presidential nomination. We watched the news and went to bed.

The next morning, when I arose, Fred was watching a newscast, and the news was all about the assassination of Bobby Kennedy. Many pictures were shown of Bobby Kennedy lying lifeless on the floor. This time my thoughts turned to values. My question was, "Is being president worth the price?" When we have to pay the price, our thoughts turn to the worthwhileness of the cause.

If leadership were only a position, the cost could be far too great. Fortunately for us, we serve the greatest and most worthwhile cause of all. We do our work with eternity in view. We set our sights on winning people to Christ, on making disciples, on training people to serve, and on ministries of compassion.

Second, perhaps courage is the one characteristic which is needed most in meeting the challenge of leadership. As Wolff points out, courage comes from the French word *coeur*, meaning heart (1970, 47). It takes a lot of "heart" or courage to be a leader. As Wolff states: "A leader needs courage because leadership involves risk. Courage is necessary to overcome the anguish, the loneliness, perhaps the ridicule and the rejection. The possibility of failure often looms large" (1970, 47). Wolff adds these comments:

> In his last letter addressed to a leader of the church, Paul reminds Timothy to rekindle the gift of God which is in him "for God did not give us a spirit of timidity but a spirit of power and love and self-control" (II Tim. 1:7). Positively expressed, God gives us courage, heart—and this must be preeminently so in the case of a leader. (1970, 47)

Third, centuries before Christ, Moses said to the Lord, "If your presence does not go with us, do not lead us up from here" (Exod. 33:15). The presence of God is absolutely essential for us. We cannot meet the challenges of leadership without the presence of God.

We are blessed by the promises of God with regard to His presence. Before His death, Jesus declared, "I will ask the Father, and He will give you another Helper, that He may be with you forever" (John 14:16). Then, following His resurrection, Jesus said, "and lo, I am with you always, even to the end of the age" (Matt. 28:20). We do not face the challenge alone!

Fourth, we must know the rewards of leadership. Some day we will be with Christ. This will be our highest reward. We will participate in the timeless exaltation and praise of our Lord! Only believers in Christ will experience this. Then we will hear Christ's voice of approval for all that we have done. We will receive the "imperishable" wreath for our victory in running the race (1 Cor. 9:25). Apart from this, the highest reward will be the harvest of our efforts. All of those that we have influenced toward Jesus will be there. What a joy that will be!

Conclusion

Sometimes leadership involves position, honor, and power, but the indispensable ingredient in great leadership is service. When we serve, we are a leader even if only in the sense of leading in service. We may lead in other ways also, but servant leadership demands service. Individually and organizationally, we must focus on what meets the needs of the people we serve.

We must pay the price of leadership. Christian leadership is no exception to this rule. As Christian leaders we must understand the required steps to leadership. We must know that leadership takes us along the pathway of humility. The needs of men, the commands of our Lord, and the urgency of the hour all demand men and women who will step forward and pay the price of leadership.

CHAPTER FOUR

THE LEADER'S CONFIDENCE

Introduction

Jesus defined greatness in terms of service. We are great when we serve, and servanthood is a position in itself. Other positions may derive from service, but the service is itself valuable. One can be *ahead* of others in service without being *a head* or *the head* of a group. In the sense of being *ahead* of others, as well as being *a head* or *the head*, a person can be a true leader.

When we define leadership in terms of being *a head* or *the head*, then matters such as influence with people, setting of goals, gathering people around those goals, and implementing them come into focus. However, given what Jesus says about greatness, we have concluded that service is the indispensable quality in leaders who are *a head* or *the head* of an organization.

Jesus challenged the disciples to weigh the cost of becoming great or becoming first. As we have seen, leadership exacts a price. Anyone who aspires to leadership should count the cost. When the cost of leading is counted, some will pull back, but many will forge ahead. A true leader will learn to put service first. No matter what other motivation may enter in, by an act of the will, service will have priority.

James and John responded to Jesus' challenge by quickly declaring, "We are able." They were confident that they could pay the price. Jesus saw that they did not know the full extent of the cost. They would come later to a full knowledge of the cost. Their comment raises the issue of the leader's confidence or the role of confidence in leadership.

Once again, I will present the entire leadership story that has captivated our attention, the story in Matthew 20:20-28. Our specific focus in this chapter is on the comment of the disciples in verse 22b that "We are able."

[20]Then the mother of the sons of Zebedee came to Jesus with her sons, bowing down and making a request of Him.
[21]And He said to her, "What do you wish?"

She said to Him, "Command that in Your kingdom these two sons of mine may sit one on Your right and one on Your left."

²²But Jesus answered, "You do not know what you are asking. Are you able to drink the cup that I am about to drink?" They said to Him, "We are able."

²³He said to them, "My cup you shall drink; but to sit on My right and on *My* left, this is not Mine to give, but it is for those for whom it has been prepared by My Father."

²⁴And hearing *this*, the ten became indignant with the two brothers.

²⁵But Jesus called them to Himself and said, "You know that the rulers of the Gentiles lord it over them, and *their* great men exercise authority over them.

²⁶It is not this way among you, but whoever wishes to become great among you shall be your servant.

²⁷and whoever wishes to be first among you shall be your slave;

²⁸just as the Son of Man did not come to be served, but to serve, and to give His life a ransom for many."

We will include, but not limit, our discussion to the confidence leaders have that they can pay the price of leadership. Rather than limit the discussion, we will discuss many aspects of confidence in leading. Our topics will focus on (1) self-confidence and confidence in others, (2) mitigating extremes in self-confidence, (3) the role of faith in Christ, and (4) how to develop confidence.

Confidence

An important factor in leadership is self-confidence. The leader's self-confidence will vary depending on the situations that he faces. For example, a local church leader who is very confident in teaching a class, might not be as confident when trying to expand the attendance. However, the leader in all situations is expected to be confident in what he or she is doing.

First, according to Titus, a primary assumption in politics is self-significance. He holds that:

This [self-significance] manifests itself in such aspects as self-awareness, self-confidence, and self-interest. The words "I," "I exist," "I can do," "I will," and "I count," are vital definite statements of fact as far as most individuals are concerned and, as such, are taken-for-granted situations in the minds of most people. If a person drops below this level of awareness or has never attained to such a level, he is of little concern as an active element in the field of politics. (1950)

According to Ross and Hendry, Cecil A. Gibb found that leadership and self-confidence were highly correlated (1957, 57-58). They quote the following conclusion by Gibb: "The general implication of these findings is that leaders, more or less consistently, rate higher than followers in self-confidence or self-assurance. A person who believes in himself gives the impression that he has the skill, power, or ability which will enable him to solve the problem in hand" (1954, 886). When leaders have confidence, they can be relaxed, be themselves, and speak with assurance. Clearly, this helps them lead.

Second, confidence has great power and is contagious. Many people will respond to the leader who confidently faces problems and poses solutions. Bogardus reminds us that "Franklin D. Roosevelt commanded many new followers as soon as he became President by the confidence which he literally radiated throughout the whole United States in his radio addresses. No matter how troublesome the issue, his voice came over the radio breathing an assurance that drew thousands if not millions to him" (1934, 212-213). When a person is in a position of leadership, he or she is expected to act with confidence. When a leader lacks confidence, few will follow.

Third, both introverts and extroverts can act with confidence. However, it seems that self-confidence often comes very naturally to the extrovert and, along with this, some feelings of superiority. The introvert, in contrast, may have a more difficult time being self-confident. He can be self-confident, but he may demonstrate that self-confidence in a different way. For example, he may study a problem and its solutions and have great confidence in his findings. However, he may not exude self-confidence in the same way as the extrovert in his presentation.

Fourth, Wolff discusses the question, "Can a leader be humble?" (1970, 13-16). He declares, "Legitimate ambition, the desire to be a leader, does not run counter to true humility" (1970, 13). He then explains that, "Evangelical humility is based on and conformed to the real circumstances and character of man. The views which the humble man entertains of himself and of his condition are an exact reflection of his situation. The humble estimate is the true one" (1970, 14). Confidence can and should be well-seasoned with humility. Humility and self-confidence need not be contradictory. Confidence helps a person achieve good things; humility puts both the person and the achievement in proper perspective. As in many things, balance is the key word.

Fifth, before leaving the subject of confidence, we should consider the leader's confidence in others. A leader shows confidence in others as well as himself. Studies show that the person who expects more from his subordinates because he believes in their abilities will actually get more. We want to do well when others believe we can. As James M. Kouzes and Barry Z. Posner maintain:

> Indeed, when we ask people to describe exemplary leaders, they consistently talk about people who have been able to bring out the best in them. This is one of the defining characteristics of a leader, one of the things that make constituents willing to be led: that person has our best interests at heart and wants us to be as successful as possible. Leading others requires that leaders have high expectations about what people can accomplish. (1997, 272)

We show confidence in people by delegating matters to them and empowering them to do certain tasks. Some companies make it a policy to push decision-making out to the arena where transactions take place. Airline ticket agents, for example, seem to have considerable authority. Doing this requires putting confidence in people to do the right thing.

Mitigating Extremes

With regard to confidence, two extremes hamper leadership: (1) too much confidence and (2) too little confidence. Many people are put off by these extremes. We must learn to mitigate the extremes that sometimes develop in our lives. We can lessen the harsh impact of these negative developments.

First, let us consider overconfidence and its results. The case of the disciples is very interesting. We will begin with them and their attitude. Then, we will discuss other leaders and the importance of toning down overconfidence in ourselves and putting our full confidence in God.

One. Many commentators believe that the disciples were overconfident. According to them, their ready answer, "We are able," was the first evidence they were not able. Also, not knowing all that was coming, they could not have been fully prepared to answer. It appears to me that the disciples were over-confident in their own strength.

Although the disciples were overconfident, there is a positive side to their answer. Concerning this point, Hendriksen maintains that, "On the favorable side we can at least credit them with a considerable measure of loyalty to their Master. Nevertheless, the future would prove that they were at this moment too self-confident" (1973, 746). Similarly, Smart suggests that, "When James and John answered 'We are able,' Jesus honored their confession and assured them that in the future they would indeed share to the full his mission, his Spirit, and his sufferings" (1979, 291).

The disciples would soon be tested. A blow was struck to their self-confidence the night Jesus was taken prisoner in the Garden of Gethsemane. Earlier in the evening, Jesus said to the disciples, "You will all fall away because of Me this night" (Matt. 26:31). Peter boldly replied, "*Even* though all may fall away because of You, I will never fall away" (Matt. 26:33). Then Jesus said, "Truly I say to you that this *very* night, before a rooster crows, you will deny Me three times" (Matt. 26:34). Peter was the boldest speaker among them, but he was soon to fall.

Jesus did not rebuke James and John for their claim that they were able to drink the cup that Jesus was about to drink. He knows that they, indeed, will pay the price. Peter failed, but he came back, enabled by the Spirit, as one of the strongest witnesses in the early church. Over time, all the others, except Judas, stood the test! They fully committed themselves to Christ.

Two. Other leaders, in addition to the disciples, sometimes are hampered by an attitude of over-confidence. Overconfidence often is a prelude to defeat. We see this in the sports world. A team that is over-confident may not respect its opponent enough. As a result, the overconfident team may not do its best. Many championship teams have their toughest years after winning. Some of their desire and dedication is lost. They begin to feel they can maintain championship quality play without paying the prices of discipline and preparation.

Sometimes when leaders are overconfident, they lose their followers. They begin to reveal their sense of superiority. However, their programs and ways may be presumptuous and superficial.

Unless realism is maintained, people will not believe them and will not continue following.

Second, some leaders lack confidence. Too little confidence and a sense of inferiority tend to go together. According to Thomas A. Harris, Adler held the theory that feelings of inferiority were the basis of man's struggle in life. He claimed that the child, by virtue of his small size and helplessness, inevitably considered himself inferior to the adult figures in his environment (1969, 67). This may be true in some cases, but there are also other reasons for feelings of inferiority. When people have feelings of inferiority, it can hamper, to some degree, their ability to lead. Fortunately, feelings of inferiority can be overcome.

It has been my privilege to work with many leaders in church circles. In public life, they manifest enormous confidence and self-assurance. When you get to know them better, you discover that many of them feel inferior about something. They may feel inferior about their education, personal appearance, lack of ministry gifts, or some other factor. In spite of these feelings, they have learned to live and function with both their strengths and weaknesses. They have sufficiently overcome their feelings of inferiority to function effectively.

Third, balance is an important factor in leading. We can identify two clusters of traits with regard to confidence. One cluster may include overconfidence, feelings of superiority, and extroversion. Another cluster may include lack of confidence, feelings of inferiority and introversion. As I have noted above, an introvert may have confidence even though he expresses it in a different way. In any case, an effective effort draws in a balanced way from people with all of these traits.

The apostle Paul tells us: "For through the grace given to me I say to everyone among you not to think more highly of himself than he ought to think; but to think so as to have sound judgment, as God has allotted to each a measure of faith" (Rom. 12:3). Here, we observe both sides of the coin: (1) we should not think too highly of ourselves and (2) we should recognize that each of us has a measure of faith. Although Paul does not say it, because of our measure of faith, we ought not to think too lowly of ourselves either.

Faith in Christ

When believers speak about confidence, they know that they are fully dependent upon God. Because of this, we need to consider several points relative to our faith in Christ.

First, for the Christian leader, humility and confidence meet through faith in Christ. Inferiority feelings are overcome, and superiority feelings are mitigated when we place ourselves in Him. When we are in Christ, the focus is taken off of us and is put on Him. We simply become the instruments of His mercy to a lost world.

Second, the Christian leader must be confident in Christ. Paul knew that His strength was in the Lord. He wrote the following message to the Philippians (4:12-13):

> [12]I know how to get along with humble means, and I also know how to live in prosperity; in any and every circumstance I have learned the secret of being filled and going hungry, both of having abundance and suffering need.
> [13]I can do all things through Him who strengthens me.

Paul was able to face all kinds of circumstances through Christ who strengthened him. In verse 12, Paul mentions several specific circumstances, but I believe this truth applies to all aspects of our lives and ministries. It applies to our ministries as well as to our physical circumstances. Whatever difficult situation we face, we can overcome in His strength. Without Him, we might fail, but with Him we will be victorious.

Like all other people, Paul had weaknesses, but he did not let these deter him from his task. Even with his weaknesses, he had confidence in God. He was given a thorn in the flesh to keep him from being exalted (2 Cor. 12:7). Concerning this weakness, and others, he declared: "Therefore I am well content with weaknesses, with insults, with distresses, with persecutions, with difficulties, for Christ's sake; for when I am weak, then I am strong" (2 Cor. 12:10).

Some people said Paul was weak in speech and personal presence. While Paul was writing to the Corinthians, he addressed this point. In his reply, Paul reveals his confidence. He said (2 Cor. 10:10-11):

> [10]For they say, "His letters are weighty and strong, but his personal presence is unimpressive and his speech contemptible."

[11]Let such a person consider this, that what we are in word by letters when absent, such persons *we are* also in deed when present.

Third, the Christian leader must have a sense of dependence on the Lord. The Psalmist wrote: "Some *boast* in chariots and some in horses, but we will boast in the name of the Lord, our God" (Ps. 20:7). Similarly, Paul declared: "BUT HE WHO BOASTS IS TO BOAST IN THE LORD. For it is not he who commends himself that is approved, but he whom the Lord commends" (2 Cor. 10:17-18).[1]

The prophet Micah spoke of the source of his power with these words: "On the other hand I am filled with power—With the Spirit of the Lord—And with justice and courage to make known to Jacob his rebellious act, Even to Israel his sin" (Micah 3:8). Confronting Israel was a daunting task, but Micah was undaunted because of the presence and power of the Spirit. We have analogous words from the prophet Isaiah who said "He [God] gives strength to the weary, And to *him who* lacks might He increases power" (Isa. 40:29).

Developing Confidence

There are many factors in the development of a leader's confidence. We will consider the realization that we can change, the realistic assessment of the gifts God has given, and the role of suffering.

First, the development of confidence begins with the realization that we can change. An excellent example of this is Moses. In Acts 7:22, Stephen describes Moses as follows: "Moses was educated in all the learning of the Egyptians, and he was a man of power in words and deeds." Early in his life, Moses was well-positioned in Egypt, but he lost that standing and fled to the land of Midian. He married the daughter of Jethro who was the priest of Midian and kept his sheep (Exod. 2:15-22). After Moses had spent many years in Midian, the Lord asked him to be the deliverer of Israel. Moses objected several times before accepting this appointment.

In one of his objections, Moses expressed his lack of confidence in his speech. He said, "Please, Lord, I have never been eloquent, neither recently nor in time past, nor since You have spoken to Your servant;

---

[1] NOTE: In the NASB95 translation, quotations from the Old Testament are presented in uppercase letters.

for I am slow of speech and slow of tongue" (Exod. 4:10). Hans Finzel states:

> Still not worn down by objections, God assured Moses, "I will help you speak and will teach you what to say" (4:12). Would it not make sense that by now reticent Moses would trust God and His promises of help? God was assuring Moses that He would take care of everything; but He was also saying that He needed a man to lead His people to freedom. A side lesson of this story is the truth that God really does rely on people to do His will on earth. (1998, 8)

Acts 7:22 and Exodus 4:10 may seem to be in conflict. However, several ways have been suggested to reconcile these passages: (1) Lenski maintains that "Power is referred to and not mere readiness of tongue which explains Exod. 4:10, 15" (1934, 275). According to this view, the words of Moses were authoritative and very powerful, but not eloquent. (2) Posing another view, F. F. Bruce writes: "That he [Moses] was mighty in his words [Acts 7:22] may seem to conflict with his disclaimer of eloquence in Ex. 4:10, but the reference could be to his writings" (Bruce, 150). (3) Kenneth O. Gangel agrees with Bruce about writing, but also poses another view. He suggests the following two points:

> How interesting that Stephen should call Moses powerful in speech when Moses himself doubted his eloquence (Exod. 4:10). Two things may be in view here. First, Stephen described Moses after forty years of leadership during which time he made many eloquent pronouncements in delivering God's messages to the people. Second, Stephen might have had in mind the writing of the Pentateuch in which Moses certainly displayed great power in oral tradition until he wrote it as Scripture. (1998, 106)

It is possible, as Gangel suggests, that Stephen (Acts 7:22) may have had in mind the speeches that Moses made while leading Israel in the wilderness. In support of this, we know that Moses, in Exodus 4:10, spoke about his life before he became the deliverer of Israel. Given this information and approach, there would be no conflict between the statements of Stephen and Moses.

Henry and Richard Blackaby take a different direction in reconciling Acts 7:22 and Exodus 4:10. They emphasize that Moses had a new perspective with emphasis on God's presence. They comment as follows:

What happened? Moses used to think he was a gifted leader. Forty years later he claims he can't speak or lead! Which was correct? Both.

Moses may certainly have feared his oratorical skills had declined over the forty years of talking to four-footed audiences. But more importantly Moses came to view his skills from God's perspective. Accomplishing God's work was impossible without God's presence. Conversely Moses would learn that with every divine assignment also comes God's equipping. God would enable his servant to accomplish everything he commanded him to do. The key was not Moses' skills but Moses' surrender. (2011, 70)

The problem with the view that the oratorical skills of Moses declined "over the forty years of talking to four-footed audiences" is that Moses said "I have *never* been eloquent, neither recently nor in time past." As indicated above, he spoke these words prior to his years of leadership in the wilderness. However, it seems abundantly clear that Moses "came to view his skills from God's perspective."

Moses accepted the appointment to be the deliverer of Israel, but asked God for someone else to be the mouthpiece. Although angry with Moses, God selected Aaron to be the one who would speak. Even so, as it turned out, during the 40 years in the wilderness, Moses would speak many times.

During the wilderness experience, the Spirit of God was upon Moses in a powerful way (Num. 11:17). On one occasion, God took of the Spirit that was upon Moses and placed Him upon the seventy elders who were with him (Num. 11:25). As a result, the elders prophesied. One likely result, it appears to me, of the Spirit being upon Moses was empowered speech.

There is a strong contrast between the reticence of Moses to speak when God asked him to be the deliverer of Israel and his confidence when he spoke to Israel at the end of his ministry. Moses changed! He wanted to speak and believed his words would be effective. In the hearing of all the assembly of Israel, he said (Deut. 32:1-3):

[1]Give ear, O heavens, and let me speak; And let the earth hear the words of my mouth.

[2]"Let my teaching drop as the rain, My speech distill as the dew, As the droplets on the fresh grass, And as the showers on the herb.

[3]"For I proclaim the name of the Lord; Ascribe greatness to our God!

In verse 1, Moses appeals to the heavens to let him speak and to the earth to hear his words. Then, in the opening clause of verse 2, He says, "Let my teaching drop as the rain." The Lamsa version says, "My word shall drop as rain." This clause could be taken as a prayer, wish, command, or as a factual prediction. In any case, Moses spoke with confidence that his words could have an impact on his hearers. He was no longer reticent to speak.

Moses had lived long enough to see the mighty works of God. Thus, he proclaims the name of the Lord and ascribes greatness to God. Men will hear us when we ascribe greatness to God and demonstrate that He is the solution to their problems. No wonder Stephen said that Moses "was a man of power in words and deeds" (Acts 7:22).

Second, the Christian leader's confidence is in God, but each leader must realistically assess his gifts. We all have different gifts, and we must each use them to the fullest (Rom. 12:6-8). Also, we must realize that we are growing individuals and that our gifts will blossom as they are used. Others can help us make realistic assessments.

At times, each of us must pull back from involvement in some situations which are beyond our ability or mandate from the Lord. The Psalmist wrote: "O Lord, my heart is not proud, nor my eyes haughty; Nor do I involve myself in great matters, Or in things too difficult for me" (Ps. 131:1). In some cases, we are well advised to follow his example.

Third, Tead makes an insightful statement about the role of suffering in the leader's developing faith and sense of confidence. He writes:

Again, the experience of great leaders suggests a further element too vital to be ignored. No accounting for the strength of their inner resources can fail to appreciate the part that suffering has played in their development. They have seemed in many instances to discover their faith and power in meeting and overcoming opposition of one sort or another, in surmounting seemingly insurmountable obstacles, in refusing to admit defeat, in sacrificing to the limit for their cause. In a word they have suffered in the depths of their being as one of the prices paid for the superb confidence and courage they were gradually able to manifest. (1935, 265)

Conclusion

When Jesus asked James and John if they could endure the suffering that He would experience, they answered, "We are able." Jesus did not rebuke them for their overly confident reply. Rather, He told them that they indeed would suffer. As we know, on other occasions, Jesus promised to be with the disciples and promised the help of the Holy Spirit. They could be confident when they placed their full faith in Jesus.

Let us remember that we are in Christ. Paul wrote: "For you have died and your life is hidden with Christ in God" (Col. 3:3). Remembering this, we can be filled with His confidence. The disciples were not as ready to suffer for Christ as they thought they were. They were not ready to drink the cup He had to drink. However, in the end, they stood the test. With the help of the Lord, they came through in victory. We must remember that because He is able, we are able. We are not alone in our mission. Christ will be with us each step of the way.

CHAPTER FIVE

THE LEADER'S DESTINY

Introduction

We have been studying one of the great leadership stories in the Bible. This story, found in Matthew 20:20-28, touches on many vital issues in leadership. At this point I will present the entire passage and then focus in this chapter on verse 23.

[20]Then the mother of the sons of Zebedee came to Jesus with her sons, bowing down and making a request of Him.

[21]And He said to her, "What do you wish?"
She said to Him, "Command that in Your kingdom these two sons of mine may sit one on Your right and one on Your left."

[22]But Jesus answered, "You do not know what you are asking. Are you able to drink the cup that I am about to drink?" They said to Him, "We are able."

[23]He said to them, "My cup you shall drink; but to sit on My right and on *My* left, this is not Mine to give, but it is for those for whom it has been prepared by My Father."

[24]And hearing *this*, the ten became indignant with the two brothers.

[25]But Jesus called them to Himself and said, "You know that the rulers of the Gentiles lord it over them, and *their* great men exercise authority over them.

[26]It is not this way among you, but whoever wishes to become great among you shall be your servant.

[27]and whoever wishes to be first among you shall be your slave;

[28]just as the Son of Man did not come to be served, but to serve, and to give His life a ransom for many."

The phrase "for whom it has been prepared by My Father" stirs our curiosity and gives us our topic for this chapter which is, "The Leader's Destiny." A leader's understanding of his place and role often includes a sense of destiny. Writing about leaders in general, Tead said, "the greatest leaders have been sustained by a belief that they were in some way instruments of destiny, that they tapped hidden reserves of power, that they truly lived as they tried to live in harmony with some greater, more universal purpose or intention in the world" (1935, 264).

Winston Churchill is an example of how great leaders have a sense of destiny. He became Prime Minister on May 10, 1940. Concerning the world situation at the time, the times were difficult. According to Robert Morrison, Churchill "often said he would not call those dark days, but stern days" (2011, American Thinker). Morrison then describes how stern the days were.

> The German army, the Wehrmacht, had just overrun Belgium, the Netherlands, and Luxembourg and was driving deeply into France. The small British Expeditionary Force was being cut off and reduced to a small pocket around Dunkirk, on the English Channel. The German air force, the Luftwaffe, was spreading terror among the citizens of bombed-out towns and villages and strafing panicked civilians as they clogged the roads—making the roads impassable to French and British relief columns. . . . With Britain's troops stranded on the French coast, Hitler might have parachuted 10,000 crack commandos into the heart of London and taken the country by shock and awe.

Next, Morrison cites what Churchill said about his election to the position of Prime Minister and his sense of destiny. Churchill believed that he was prepared for the position and felt that it was his destiny to be the Prime Minister. Morrison quotes Churchill as follows:

> Thus, then, on the night of the 10th of May, at the outset of this mighty battle, I acquired the chief power in the State. ... At last I had the authority to give directions over the whole scene. I felt as if I were walking with destiny, and that all my past life had been but a preparation for this hour and for this trial. . . . I thought I knew a good deal about it all, and I was sure I should not fail. Therefore, although impatient for the morning, I slept soundly and had no need for cheering dreams. Facts are better than dreams. (www.americanthinker.com)

Very often Christian leaders, as well as secular, have a strong sense of destiny. When we apply this to Christian leaders, several questions arise: Does God have a plan for some leaders? Does He have a plan for everyone? Are there alternatives in the plan? Does the plan permit freedom of the will? What can we do to fulfill the plan? These are significant and searching questions.

Our answers will be influenced by our views on free will and determinism. Therefore, we will discuss (1) controlled freedom, (2) controlled freedom applied to leadership positions, (3) controlled freedom applied to greatness, and (4) a suggested course of action. This lesson should be an encouragement to leaders as they fulfil their destiny.

Controlled Freedom

When we discuss destiny, we must consider freedom and determinism or, to put it another way, man's free will and God's sovereignty. Here we will discuss the problem we encounter when considering free will and God's control. Then we will focus our attention on the Biblical emphasis, a presentation of my view, and some brief comments about destiny.

First, both theology and philosophy grapple with the problems we encounter when we consider freedom and determinism. Many thinkers have supported the idea of freedom or free will. Herman Horne, as I elsewhere reported, held that the will is man's mind, or entire consciousness, in action and that the will is free because the mind is free. By directing its attention, the mind can select the strongest motive (1966). Determinism, on the other hand, is the view that the universe operates by the laws of cause and effect and that all things are determined. When held in its extreme form, this view allows for no freedom. Similarly, when freedom is overemphasized, the role of determinism is not recognized.

Both determinism and freedom views have their strengths and weaknesses. The advantage of determinism is that it readily accounts for heredity, environment, prophecy, foreknowledge, and the sovereignty of God. However, determinism faces the problem of what to say about human freedom, responsibility, and personal initiative. The views that emphasize freedom have the advantage in treating free will, personal responsibility, and initiative. They confront problems with regard to heredity, environment, prophecy, foreknowledge, and God's sovereignty. Because of these strengths and weaknesses, some tension between the views always remains.

Jesus recognized the influence of heredity, environment, and the will on our lives. As evidence of this, I would cite Matthew 19:12 where Jesus declared: "For there are eunuchs who were born that way from their mother's womb; and there are eunuchs who were made eunuchs by men; and there are also eunuchs who made themselves eunuchs for the sake of the kingdom of heaven."

Jesus was interacting with the Pharisees about marriage and divorce. According to Walter Bauer, the Greek word for eunuchs (*eunouchoi, εὐνοῦχοι*) can refer to castrated men, to men who are not castrated but are incapable of marrying and begetting children, and to those who abstain from marriage without being impotent (1957, 323-324). Although these subjects are not my topics here, I mention this passage because, as others have noted, it has implications for the forces that influence our lives.

The point I want to make is that in Matthew 19:12, Jesus recognizes the influence of heredity, environment, and the will: (1) We recognize the role of heredity when men "were born" eunuchs. (2) When men "were made" eunuchs by other men, we regard these other men as a part of the environment. (3) Those men who "made themselves" eunuchs, do so by an act of their will.

Second, the Bible emphasizes both free will and the sovereignty of God. Sometimes, we can find both emphases side-by-side in the same verse of Scripture. For example, we read in Philippians 2:12-13, "So then, my beloved, just as you have always obeyed, not as in my presence only, but now much more in my absence, work out your salvation with fear and trembling; for it is God who is at work in you, both to will and to work for *His* good pleasure." We are to "work out" our salvation, but it is God who is "at work in you."

The Bible teaches both these truths without attempting to fully reconcile them. While writing about divine sovereignty and human responsibility in evangelism, J. I. Packer posits that:

> What the Bible does is to assert both truths side by side in the strongest and most unambiguous terms as two ultimate facts; this, therefore, is the position that we must take in our own thinking. C. H. Spurgeon was once asked if he could reconcile these two truths to each other. "I wouldn't try," he replied; "I never reconcile friends." Friends?--yes *friends*. This is the point we have to grasp." (1961, 35)

Third, **a**long with others, I do not believe that we can fully reconcile freedom and determinism. A part of the problem is that we approach the subject with a finite mind and from a human point of view. Free will and determinism are fully reconciled only in the mind of God. Freedom and determinism at best paradoxical to us, but they are completely "friendly" in God's mind.

Even though we cannot fully reconcile freedom and determinism, we can observe and accept the Biblical data with regard to this issue. It helps me to put all this data under the general heading of a term that I have coined—"controlled freedom." I say "freedom" because the universe is alive, full of interaction, and includes freedom and moral responsibility. Then, I say "controlled" because God is in charge and has ultimate control over all things. This view, like others, does not fully reconcile free will and determinism, but it does give us some practical handles to cope with the two truths and apply them to our lives.

The starting point of controlled freedom is that God "works all things after the counsel of His will" (Eph. 1:11). Given this, the next step is to determine "how" He works. From our human perspective, some things are undetermined. Other things are progressively determined, and still others are predetermined. Among the things that God has predetermined, one is to allow some things to be progressively determined and others to be undetermined. In all things, God is at work! I say "from our human perspective" because this is the only way we can see them. We are not God and cannot see them completely as He sees them.

The strength of controlled freedom is that it accepts the Biblical data at face value without attempting to reconcile every point. Critics would ask, "How can some things be determined without all things being determined?" We must not overlook the fact that God does the miraculous. He can bypass time and preconditions to create what He wants. For example, He could create a tree with rings in it! Our finite minds cannot fully comprehend this. Even though the concept of controlled freedom does not fully escape all philosophical problems, it is a helpful way to include all the data of the Bible.

Fourth, now we can ask the question, "What is destiny?" By our own choices, we shape much of our lives. The word "destiny," however, takes us beyond our own choices to those things which are being progressively determined and which have been predetermined. When we have a sense of destiny, it brings in forces outside of us that influence our lives. When we are destined, we are not totally masters of our own fate. The most important factor in all this is that we are living in harmony with the will of God. By living in accordance with His will, we relate to a purpose and plan far greater than ourselves.

Controlled Freedom Applied to Positions

When we apply "controlled freedom" to positions of leadership, several points can be made. We will discuss positions that are already allocated, positions that are unallocated, and the fact that God is in control.

First, some positions, both in heaven and on earth, are already allocated. Because they may be allocated either by foreknowledge or predestination, the term *allocated* helps us avoid, to some degree, the controversy over these topics. God has made a decision as to who will occupy some places of leadership. Because the timing of the allocation may be during one's life, we may also include those allocations that are "progressively determined." Several points are important.

One. The question arises as to who will sit on the right hand and the left hand of Jesus in His kingdom. Jesus said, "but to sit on My right and on *My* left, this is not Mine to give, but it is for those for whom it has been prepared by My Father" (verse 23). Lenski explains: "Who will occupy these seats Jesus does not intimate; perhaps this knowledge was withheld from Jesus during his state of humiliation. Hence we cannot be certain whether only two will occupy those seats; perhaps more will be seated there" (1943, 789). Christ's statement seems to suggest that individuals are meant, but we might think also of categories of people, such as people who are faithful.

Barnes raises the issue of whether or not Jesus is involved in bestowing rewards on the disciples. His proposed translation of verse 23 is different from the NASB and many other versions. He states his view as follows:

> The translation of this place evidently does not express the sense of the original. The translation expresses the idea that Jesus has nothing to do with bestowing rewards on his followers. This is at variance with the uniform testimony of the Scriptures. Mat. xxv, 31-40; Jn. v. 22-30. The correct translation of the passage would be, "'To sit on my right hand and on my left is not mine to give, *except to those* for whom it is prepared by my Father.' The passage thus declares that *Christ* would give rewards to his

followers, but only to such as should be entitled to them according to the *purpose of his Father."* (1832, 209)

As Barnes maintains, Jesus is involved in bestowing rewards, including positions of honor, but the translation in the NASB does not preclude the role of Jesus. Jesus says that the Father determines who will sit on His right and left hands, not who will bestow the honor.

Even though the occupants of some positions are predetermined, we should not overlook the human aspect of their exaltation. Charles R. Erdman comments: "The rewards indeed may be given at last by Christ, but they will not be given independently of real desert; for time and eternity, the highest places in His Kingdom are prepared for those by whom they are deserved" (1920, 162). Thus the concepts of rewards and destiny do not exclude human responsibility.

Two. A study of Biblical leaders reveals much. Some of them were either predetermined or progressively determined to take their roles in leadership. They were chosen of God for special roles in the kingdom of God.

David became king over Israel when he was thirty years old and reigned for forty years. At one point in his reign, according to 2 Samuel 5:12, "David realized that the Lord had established him as king over Israel, and that He had exalted his kingdom for the sake of His people Israel." Here, David realizes that He is, indeed, living according to God's will. God has placed him in a place of leadership.

We think also of Jeremiah. Here is the word of the Lord spoken to Jeremiah, the prophet: "Before I formed you in the womb I knew you, and before you were born I consecrated you; I have appointed you a prophet to the nations" (Jer. 1:5). It could be argued that God's appointment was based on foreknowledge. This softens, to some degree, the idea of predestination. However, this would only change the way in which the determination was made. It was still known to God, in advance, that Jeremiah would be a prophet.

Another example is John the Baptist. Zacharias and Elizabeth had no children, so Zacharias prayed for a child. The angel of the Lord appeared to Zacharias and assured him that Elizabeth would bear a son. The angel instructed Zacharias to call the son John and said, "For he will be great in the sight of the Lord; and he will drink no wine or liquor, and he will be filled with the Holy Spirit, while yet in his mother's womb. And he will turn back many of the sons of Israel to the Lord their God" (Luke 1:15-16).

The apostle Paul affords us another example. He expressed this thought to the Galatians: "But when God, who had set me apart, *even from my mother's womb*, and called me through His grace, was pleased to reveal His Son in me, that I might preach Him among the Gentiles, I did not immediately consult with flesh and blood, nor did I go up to Jerusalem to those who were apostles before me; but I went away to Arabia, and returned once more to Damascus" (Gal. 1:15-16). Throughout his ministry, Paul had this sense of destiny about his ministry. No doubt this sustained him through many difficult times.

Second, other positions appear to be unallocated; that is, we fill them through very human processes such as elections. Of course, this does not exclude the activity of God in guiding us as we vote. It just moves the selection process in the direction of human activity. As an example, let us observe the early church making a choice of someone to take the place of Judas. In Acts 1:23-26 we read:

23So they put forward two men, Joseph called Barsabbas (who was also called Justus), and Matthias.
24And they prayed and said, "You, Lord, who know the hearts of all men, show which one of these two You have chosen
25to occupy this ministry and apostleship from which Judas turned aside to go to his own place."
26And they drew lots for them, and the lot fell to Matthias; and he was added to the eleven apostles.

As another example, because of problems in the church community, it was deemed advisable to select men to do some administrative tasks. They are sometimes called the first "deacons." The story of this event is found in Acts 6:1-6.

1Now at this time while the disciples were increasing *in number*, a complaint arose on the part of the Hellenistic *Jews* against the *native* Hebrews, because their widows were being overlooked in the daily serving *of food*.
2So the twelve summoned the congregation of the disciples and said, "It is not desirable for us to neglect the word of God in order to serve tables.

³"Therefore, brethren, select from among you seven men of good reputation, full of the Spirit and of wisdom, whom we may put in charge of this task.

⁴"But we will devote ourselves to prayer and to the ministry of the word."

⁵The statement found approval with the whole congregation; and they chose Stephen, a man full of faith and of the Holy Spirit, and Philip, Prochorus, Nicanor, Timon, Parmenas and Nicolas, a proselyte from Antioch.

⁶And these they brought before the apostles; and after praying, they laid their hands on them.

Third, whatever process God uses, or allows, He is in control. The freedom that we have operates within the context of God's control. Speaking through Isaiah, the prophet, God said (Isa. 46:9-10):

⁹"Remember the former things long past, for I *am* God, and there is no other; I am God, and there is no one like me,

¹⁰Declaring the end from the beginning and from ancient times things which have not been done, saying, 'My purpose will be established, and I will accomplish all My good pleasure'."

Yes, God is in control. This principle applies to being put into positions of leadership, just as it does to the rest of life. We can learn much from Psalm 75:4-7:

⁴"I said to the boastful, 'Do not boast,' and to the wicked, 'Do not lift up the horn;

⁵Do not lift up your horn on high, do not speak with insolent pride.'"

⁶For not from the east, nor from the west, nor from the desert *comes* exaltation;

⁷But God is the Judge; He puts down one, and exalts another.

Sometimes God reveals the destiny of leaders ahead of time, but very often He does not. Because He does not, all leaders simply have to learn to trust Him. He will lead them down the path He has in mind for them.

Controlled Freedom Applied to Greatness

Jesus recognized that the disciples wanted to be great, so He showed them the way. It would be a costly way and one that involved their own personal responsibility in a very striking manner. So how does controlled freedom apply to greatness?

First, when we speak of greatness, we have the sense that this attribute is open to all. When Jesus responded to Salome and the disciples concerning their desires, He spoke in indeterminate terms. His remarks were addressed to "whoever wishes to become great among you." The word "whoever" opens the door to anyone. We can conclude that everyone who would meet Christ's criterion can be great.

Second, Jesus made service the essential criterion of greatness. This means that "servant" is itself a position. We have the position of servant when we serve! Sometimes the position of servant is not crowded with applicants. The "position open" sign is in heaven's window beckoning us to apply. Even though the position is open, we can still have a sense of destiny in filling it. We are sons of God and are chosen to be His servants.

Third, paradoxically, service often leads to positions of leadership. Many writers hold that leaders are chosen by a group when they fill at least two important functions: (1) they contribute to the group's achieving of certain goals, and (2) they contribute to the satisfaction of the group's emotional needs. Sometimes group goals dominate, but at other times the emotional needs are more important. In any case, serving the needs of the people clearly has an impact on being chosen for leadership.

A Course of Action

Given the impact of both the human and the divine upon us as leaders, what should we do? What should be our course of action? When we consider what we must do, the presupposition is that we are free to do it.

First, we should build on the basis that God has chosen us for our place in the Kingdom. Jesus said, "You did not choose Me, but I chose you, and appointed you, that you should go and bear fruit, and that your fruit should remain, that whatever you ask of the Father in My name, He may give it to you" (John 15:16). As chosen vessels of God, we will bear the fruit of righteousness, and also we will be fruitful in our witness. Many will come to know Christ through our witness. With the knowledge that God has chosen us, we can serve wherever He puts us.

Second, let us give the highest attention to service. Service in the kingdom of God has priority. It is the element without which we cannot be great! Through service, we will help the group to get the job done, and we will contribute to their emotional well- being and health. When we do this, our service will be well-received.

Third, as we serve, we will be able to watch our destiny unfold. My favorite verse of Scripture is Proverbs 16:9 which says, "The mind of man plans his way, But the Lord directs his steps." Sometimes we fret as we plan. We grow impatient to see what our destiny will be. Some people, even in middle age, will ask, "What am I going to be when I grow up?" With God's help, we can relax in Him and watch our destiny unfold before our eyes. God is painting our lives on the canvas even as we watch.

Fourth, as growing leaders, we always will sense some tension between the role we now have and the role we may expect, or hope, to have. Within the bounds of this tension, we can come to an acceptance of our role which will allow us to be filled with joy and enthusiasm in our work. We need not answer every question about the future in order to perform well what God has given us to do today.

Conclusion

When we think of destiny, we often think of the good things God works through us as leaders. We are grateful for these good things, but we must realize that destiny can include tests and trials as well. Once again, Jesus is our highest example.

Because Jesus would fulfil His redemptive mission in saving all who believe in Him, He had to suffer and die. His leadership exacted an enormous price. Although He suffered much, we know that He did it "for the joy set before Him" in redeeming mankind (Heb. 12:2).

According to most versions, Jesus exclaimed on the cross, "My God, My God, why hast Thou forsaken Me?" (Matt. 27:46) Whether or not Jesus was actually forsaken by the Father is debated by theologians. Many, such as Lenski, believe that He was forsaken because sin separated God the Father from Jesus when Jesus became sin for us (2 Cor. 5:21) and was made (Gal. 3:13) a curse for us (1943, 1120). Others, such as Clovis G. Chappell, hold that Jesus was not actually forsaken but felt that He was (1952, 41-43). Using the above translation, it is clear that Jesus at least felt forsaken. An amazing point is that Jesus asked why he was forsaken. He certainly knew that He would die in Jerusalem and predicted that several times, but apparently He did not anticipate feeling forsaken. This aspect of the cross was hidden from Him.

Without detracting from the customary translation, I would call attention to Lamsa's version of Matthew 27:46. His translation, which is based on Aramaic, is: "My God, my God, for this I was spared!" In addition, in the margin he has "My God, my God, This was my destiny!" These translations, too, capture a great truth. Jesus was destined to die upon the cross to atone for our sins. Because He did, He led us as no one else can! Also, we might say that He was destined to feel that He had been forsaken by God.

When difficult times come, we may feel that God has forsaken us. At such times, however, we must renew our commitment to fully trust in Him. The author of Hebrews says, "He Himself [Jesus] has said, 'I will never desert you, nor will I ever forsake you.'" Through good times and bad, Jesus is with us. Our responsibility and privilege is to fully trust in Him. When we trust in Him, we can endure all things, look forward to the future with great joy, and expect that God will be faithful to reward us in due season according to His riches. We are in His hands, and His hands are good! Let us, therefore, fulfil our destiny! When God wants us to lead, let us lead!

CHAPTER SIX

INDIGNANT COLLEAGUES

Introduction

Working with each other—this is one of our great challenges! Many problems that we may have with our colleagues revolve around questions of authority, honor, position, and other relationships. Our reactions to these problems are crucial. We can react in ways that make the problems worse, or we can respond in ways that overcome the problems. To effectively build the kingdom of God, we must overcome our problems with our colleagues.

We recognize that some conflict is inevitable and, indeed, may be necessary for growth to occur. It is important for leaders in any organization to openly discuss issues and to evaluate goals, processes, and procedures. Jim Van Yperen posits that

> Conflict offers us the chance to grow, to change our minds and to create new commitments based upon the truth God reveals. This opens the door for a whole new set of assumptions and principles for spiritual leadership . . . The first assumption is that conflict is necessary. The second is that leadership is a call and gifting. (1997, 241)

Although it is true that conflict can lead to progress and to unity, there are times when conflict is intense and has disastrous results. The conflict that we are discussing in this chapter has to do with how prospective leaders speak about their path to leadership and the potential reactions of their colleagues. As with other conflicts, it is important for everyone that they all find a basis for united thinking and action.

At least two Bible stories have an interesting bearing on this subject: (1) our text which is Matthew 20:20-28, and (2) the story of Joseph in Genesis 37:1-36. Because of their relevance, these stories form the background for this chapter. We will read our text, with a focus on verse 24, and refer to Genesis 37.

> [20]Then the mother of the sons of Zebedee came to Jesus with her sons, bowing down and making a request of Him.

²¹And He said to her, "What do you wish?"

She said to Him, "Command that in Your kingdom these two sons of mine may sit one on Your right and one on Your left."

²²But Jesus answered, "You do not know what you are asking. Are you able to drink the cup that I am about to drink?" They said to Him, "We are able."

²³He said to them, "My cup you shall drink; but to sit on My right and on *My* left, this is not Mine to give, but it is for those for whom it has been prepared by My Father."

²⁴And hearing *this*, the ten became indignant with the two brothers.

²⁵But Jesus called them to Himself and said, "You know that the rulers of the Gentiles lord it over them, and *their* great men exercise authority over them.

²⁶It is not this way among you, but whoever wishes to become great among you shall be your servant.

²⁷and whoever wishes to be first among you shall be your slave;

²⁸just as the Son of Man did not come to be served, but to serve, and to give His life a ransom for many."

The disciples were very angry with James and John because these two wanted to elevate themselves above the others. Their reaction was typical of many colleagues. Quite normally, there can be considerable resistance! Our relationships with our colleagues are very important. In this chapter, we will study (1) prospective leaders, (2) colleagues of leaders, (3) pathways to leadership, and (4) a course of action.

Prospective Leaders

There are many prospective leaders. As we consider them, we will present some thoughts on the leadership ladder, the story of James and John and the story of Joseph and his brothers.

First, many men and women will attempt to climb the leadership ladder. As long as there are people who associate with each other, there will be leaders and followers—this is a fact of life. Many men and women will attempt to ascend to leadership. Others may not actively seek leadership, but it comes their way. In one way or another, leaders will emerge.

When prospective leaders are emerging, they may well face indignant and even angry colleagues. Because of this, they do well to take a close look at what they say, when they say it, and consider how their colleagues will react. When emerging leaders speak judiciously, they often can minimize potential opposition. As we consider this topic, we will study Joseph as well as James and John.

Second, let's begin by examining the story of James and John, evaluating their motives in desiring to lead, and observing the effect of their actions. All this will be instructive for us. Speaking to Jesus, the mother of James and John made this request (verse 21): "Command that in Your kingdom these two sons of mine may sit one on Your right and one on Your left." With regard to James and John and this request, several points are relevant:

One. James and John were part of a peer group. This peer group included the twelve disciples (compare Matt. 10:2-4; Mark 3:13-19; Luke 6:13-16, and John 14:22). Peter is always mentioned first, and Judas Iscariot is always mentioned last.

This group of twelve appears to be constituted of three sub-groups. Group A included two sets of brothers, Simon Peter and Andrew and James and John, the sons of Zebedee. Andrew lived in Bethsaida. Assuming that Salome (some say Mary Clopas) was the sister of Mary, the mother of Jesus, James and John were cousins of Jesus. John wrote the Gospel of John, the three epistles bearing his name, and Revelation. Group B includes Philip, who lived in Bethsaida, Bartholomew or Nathanael, who was won to Christ by Philip, Thomas, and Matthew, the publican who wrote the gospel. Group C included James (the less) the son of Alphaeus, Simon, Lebbaeus Thaddaeus or Judas, and Judas Iscariot. The name Lebbaeus is not included in the NASB or NIV, but the KJV says, "Lebbaeus, whose surname was Thaddaeus."

James and John were young and appeared to be ambitious. Already, they had achieved, along with Peter, some status among the disciples. Their sub-group seemed to be closest to Jesus. For example, we note that Peter, James, and John were with Jesus on the Mount of Transfiguration (Matt. 17:1-7). However, James and John did not have enough status that the others clearly recognized them as above them. Now, they were asking to be raised to positions of honor, authority, and power.

Two. We cannot know with certainty what motive someone else has because motives are internal. We can only observe external behavior and surmise what the motives are. We should keep this in mind when judging others. Matthew describes the behavior of the disciples, but he does not tell us their motive. Jesus did not rebuke James and John, but he did inform them of the cost of leadership.

The other disciples believed that James and John were presumptuous and inconsiderate. No doubt, they felt some disdain for James and John. They felt that these two disciples wanted to exalt or, as we sometimes say, aggrandize themselves and their ministries. Although this is entirely possible, it also is possible that they were sincere in wanting to serve better, but they were unwise in knowing how to do this. The most likely conclusion, as I see it, is that their motives were somewhat mixed. In any case, Jesus did not condemn them.

Three. The effect, or impact, of the actions of James and John was not surprising. The result was that their colleagues were indignant. Instinctively, peers often react to group members who are trying to take authority. The tendency for the peers is to try to impede the progress of the offending members toward leadership.

Third, we will follow the same approach to the story of Joseph. We will consider the story, evaluate the actions of Joseph, and observe the result of what he did. The story of Joseph is right on point. Friends, relatives, and co-workers may be offended by one who is rising to leadership.

One. Joseph was seventeen years of age when this story begins. He was the son of Jacob's old age (Gen. 37:1-4). Joseph was pasturing the flock with his brothers and took a bad report of their activities back to their father. His father loved him more than all his brothers and gave him a multicolored coat. As a result, his brothers hated him.

Then Joseph had a dream, told it to his brothers, and they hated him more (Gen. 37:5-8). In his dream, they were binding sheaves in the field, and Joseph's sheaf rose up and stood erect while the others sheaves bowed down to his. This caused his brothers to ask (verse 8): "Are you actually going to reign over us?" In anticipation of this possibility, their hatred for him grew even stronger.

Joseph then had still another dream (Gen. 37:9-11). The sun, moon, and stars were bowing down to him. Joseph told this dream to his father and to his brothers. Because the dream indicated that Joseph's father and mother, as well as his brothers, would bow down to him, his father rebuked him. His brothers were jealous, but his father "kept the saying *in mind*" (verse 11).

Two. As we evaluate Joseph's actions, we should remember that Joseph merely reported the dreams as they were revealed to him. Although the text does not say so, it seems clear that the dreams were from the Lord. We are not told what Joseph's motive was in reporting the dreams. We are told, however, how the disciples reacted. They were very negative and resentful. As the story unfolds, we begin to feel that Joseph was unwise in telling what he had dreamed. However, at the end of the story, we realize how much good God brought out of what appeared to be unwise actions (Gen. 50:20).

Three. As we have seen, the brothers of Joseph became very angry over his dreams and hated him more. They plotted against him, threw him into a pit, and sold him to some Ishmaelite traders who were passing by. They, in turn, sold him in Egypt to Potiphar, Pharaoh's officer, the captain of the bodyguard. This was the beginning of a victorious new story which would be written! For the moment, however, the important point is that brothers sometimes become angry when one among them lets it be known that he is rising to leadership.

James and John expressed their desire to lead, and Joseph reported his dreams which identified him as the leader. The result among the peers was the same—they became very angry. The Bible says that the brothers of Joseph were jealous. Jealousy is a strong and negative force. It causes much havoc in the church.

Angry Colleagues

Our primary concern here is the reaction of the other disciples to James and John and of the brothers to Joseph. However, we will pause to note the reaction of Joseph's father as well.

First, Jacob, who was Joseph's father, was in a place of authority. Moreover, he very much loved his son Joseph. When Joseph told him his dream, Jacob rebuked him but "kept the saying in mind." One wonders how often, through the years of Joseph's absence, Jacob thought of Joseph's dreams. He did not know, of course, what was taking place in Joseph's life down in Egypt.

Second, let us consider the disciples and the brothers. The disciples "became indignant" with James and John, and the brothers of Joseph were "jealous" of him. To a degree, I suppose, these colleagues had a "right" to become angry. Many of us would have been angry, too!

However, it would appear that the motivation of the colleagues was not all that pure either. Tead states: "Feelings of jealousy toward others who may aspire to rise to the status of a leader are also encountered as subtle evidences of a desire to have self-power remain unquestioned" (1935, 215). When others rise to the "top," our own status, authority, and self-esteem may be challenged. This is enough to spark indignation or anger in our hearts.

Third, the disciples and the brothers were "hot-headed." It would have been better for them to remain "cool." The disciples should have trusted Jesus who would not award positions of honor to the undeserving. The brothers should have trusted Jacob who had their interests, as well as Joseph's, at heart. Instead, the colleagues took matters into their own hands. In so doing, they demonstrated their own flaws.

Fourth, in Matthew 20:25-28, Jesus dealt with both James and John and the other disciples. He spoke to them about authority and service. In thus replying, he provided a solution for all of them. He showed them how to solve the problem of colleagues who are indignant. We will deal with these verses in subsequent chapters.

Pathways to Leadership

As we consider pathways to leadership, several points will be of interest. These include political processes, ministry promotion, God's promotion, elections, and God's will.

First, although we would not follow many of the ways of the politicians in rising to leadership, it is interesting to observe the processes they follow. We do see, in some ways, the parallels in the church. Some things, but not all, that politicians do are legitimate in the church.

Titus deals with the way politicians rise to power: (1) Prospective leaders convert groups or clusters of people to new objectives. In so doing, they influence the units that they convert from the inside. (2) Leaders may capture an organization or country. Because they have captured the organization or country, they can control it for their own purposes. (3) Leaders may create an organization for the desired purposes. The founders of an organization, at least in the early stages, maintain control. (4) When leaders cannot control an organization through others means, conditioning is the approach. Leaders attempt to condition an organization from the outside (1950).

By way of application, (1) A pastor may become a strong leader by converting a local church to new objectives. For example, a new pastor may lead the church from the inside to become a strong missionary-sending church. (2) Using another approach, a pastor might "capture" a church. When he does this, he takes control in a stronger way. The church essentially comes under his control. (3) Many pastors have become leaders by planting a church. This is leadership through the creation of a new entity. (4) Finally, a pastor might lead by conditioning a church from the outside without directly leading the church. Many leaders have this kind of influence. Each of these approaches needs to be evaluated in given situations on its own merits.

Second, sometimes much emphasis is put on "marketing" one's ministry. Some evangelists, singers, musicians, and pastors do it. Very often, the people reached by this "marketing" will accept the ministries of those advertised. To some degree, this approach is acceptable. After all, unless people know who you are, what credentials you have, and what gifts God has given you, they may not be interested. The wise minister, however, will be careful. Although the people being reached will accept some promotion of this type, peers are notorious for rejecting it. When ministers overdo their promotion, they risk alienating their peers.

Paul was careful on this point. He wrote to the Corinthians (2 Cor. 3:1): "Are we beginning to commend ourselves again? Or do we need, as some, letters of commendation to you or from you? You are our letter, written in our hearts, known and read by all men; being manifested that you are a letter of Christ, cared for by us, written not with ink, but with the Spirit of the living God, not on tablets of stone, but on tablets of human hearts." However, Paul does not exclude all communication about his ministry. After all, his letter is itself a kind of communication.

Third, many times God clearly steps in and promotes someone to a place of leadership. When He does this, He blesses the ministry of the person promoted. For example, as the children of Israel prepared to cross the Jordan, the Lord said to Joshua, "This day I will begin to exalt you in the sight of all Israel, that they may know that just as I have been with Moses, I will be with you" (Josh. 3:7). When it is obvious that God has done the promoting, people often will follow. This does not guarantee, though, that one's peers will accept your new leadership. Close friends and colleagues often will make excuses for your success. Very happily, even such dissenters are sometimes won over.

Fourth, a common way to rise to leadership is through election. In politics, candidates make their desires known, present themselves in the best light, vote for themselves, and gather people around themselves to help promote them. It is doubtful anyone could win an election without doing this. Who would vote for someone who did not think he was the best candidate?

In the church, a different process is followed. We stress humility and promoting others. It is never wise to be seen as someone wanting a given office. As a matter of fact, many church leaders do want to be elected to certain offices, but they dare not say so. To make this public would raise the opposition of the voters. It is acceptable, however, to "allow" one's name to stand in an election process. At its worst, this whole process can be subtle and somewhat deceptive. At its best, it is an unfettered way of allowing God to bring leaders into places of responsibility.

Fifth, for Christian leaders, knowing God's will is the most important point. When we are certain that we are in His will, we can proceed with confidence. Wolff avers that "In order to do the will of God it is essential for each man to know his divinely-appointed sphere and limit (II Cor. 10:8-18), to use the gifts which he has received, to be a faithful steward, to trade with his talents, to recognize and to accept his God-given role, i.e. to shoulder his responsibility and to accomplish his task. Such ambition is not only legitimate, but a necessary ingredient of leadership" (1969, 10)

A Course of Action

With all this in focus, what must both prospective leaders and their colleagues do? It will be helpful for us to think about both groups. With regard to the first group, we will consider the ego, criticism, rungs in the ladder, helping others, and timing. Concerning colleagues, we will discuss their roles, the temptation to compare roles, Gamaliel's advice, spiritual correction, and spiritual cleansing.

First, we have many among us who are potential leaders. Many points could be made about them as they move into leadership roles, but here are a few which stand out in my mind.

One. All people have an ego. Prospective leaders, no doubt, have stronger egos than others. Given this, they must be careful how they express their egos. Tead observes that, "Broadly speaking, it is necessary that the individual's ego be enabled to express itself in ways that will not hurt others or his relation with others" (1935, 219). In our main stories, James and John and Joseph did not observe this principle. As a result, they faced opposition.

Two. Remember that some criticism will come your way. The editor of Bits and Pieces included this note: "The late David Sarnoff of RCA once said that he was just as grateful to his enemies as he was to his friends because 'in certain situations, a kick in the pants can send you even further along the path of progress than a friendly hand'" (June 1973). This is a tough idea to accept, but it is true.

Three. Prospective leaders should not be reluctant, or afraid, to put the rungs in the ladder. By that I mean they may know where they are going, but it may take a while to get there. They may have to do many things which will qualify them for their future role. The idea of apprenticeship is to prepare people for their future roles. Sometimes, prospective leaders wish to jump from where they are straight to their full stature.

Four. The apostle Paul wrote, "Let no one seek his own *good*, but that of his neighbor" (1 Cor. 10:24). We can apply this principle to the ministries of others. Those who would lead should help others lead. Paradoxical, perhaps, but true! We demonstrate the Spirit of Christ when we are helping others in their tasks. It other words, it is important to be a good follower even when you are a leader.

Five. As we have pointed out, prospective leaders must be cautious about expressing a desire for certain positions. In most cases in the church, it is better not to express their desires at all. However, over the years, this has changed somewhat. Prospective leaders in the church are much more open than they used to be about their desire to lead. With regard to their vision, a slightly different situation prevails. Prospective leaders must express their vision, but it is important that they have the right timing. If they express their vision too soon, they may encounter much opposition. Leaders must seek the Lord to know when, as well as what, to speak.

Second, we must not focus on prospective leaders alone. All of us, at times, are colleagues of leaders and, in many cases, followers as well. Not as many books are written about how to follow as how to lead, but it is important. There definitely are some principles that will help.

One. We must realize that, by God's design, each person has his role. Some of our peers may become leaders. Even when this is difficult for us, we must accept it. We must work together for the common good. To the Corinthians, Paul wrote: "For we are God's fellow workers; you are God's field, God's building" (1 Cor. 3:9). We do not work alone. We accept the roles of our brothers and work together with God to build His kingdom. We are, of course, the junior partners in this relationship.

Two. It is wise to avoid comparisons among us. Concerning himself, Paul makes this comment: "For we are not bold to class or compare ourselves with some of those who commend themselves; but when they measure themselves by themselves and compare themselves with themselves, they are without understanding" (2 Cor. 10:12). Similarly, in Galatians 6:4-5, he wrote: "But each one must examine his own work, and then he will have *reason for* boasting in regard to himself alone, and not in regard to another."

Three. Occasionally, someone will rise to prominence whose ministry seems, to us, to be unusual and perhaps suspect. Unless the ministry is clearly wrong, we are wise to wait a while before we make a final judgment. Over time, it will become clearer whether or not the ministry faithfully aligns with the Word of God. When Peter and his colleagues were called before "the Council" for their witnessing, Gamaliel gave this advice (Acts 5:38-39):

> [38]"So in the present case, I say to you, stay away from these men and let them alone, for if this plan or action is of men, it will be overthrown;
>
> [39]but if it is of God, you will not be able to overthrow them; or else you may even be found fighting against God."

The ultimate test of a ministry is not its apparent success or failure, but its harmony with God's truth. Obviously, there are times when quick action must be taken, but not always. The Spirit of God will lead us in what to do and when to do it.

Four. When God leads, you may correct a brother or sister in the Lord. You must be sure, however, that your own motives are right. Tead maintains: "Sometimes the candid friend or kindly adviser may be able to bring home to the leader the fact that his will to power has come to be his undoing. In some way he has eventually to become conscious of the fault; and by taking counsel he has to lay bare the causes or reasons why the fault has grown" (1935, 216). There are times when God calls upon us to be that candid friend.

Five. We must ask the Holy Spirit to cleanse our own spirit. Before we say much to anyone else, we must examine ourselves. It usually takes the search light of the Spirit Himself to reveal our own flaws. All too often, our own "blind spots" prevent us from seeing our weaknesses.

Conclusion

Our focus in this chapter has been on verse 24 in the Matthew story. Matthew writes, "the ten [disciples] became indignant with the two brothers." Wanting positions of honor for her two sons, the mother of James and John made a request that made the other disciples indignant. This story, along with the story of Joseph and his dreams, helps us understand how prospective leaders can stir up the indignation of their colleagues. With this understanding, we sometimes can avoid upsetting our colleagues. I say "sometimes" because some colleagues will be upset no matter what you do.

Although some conflict is virtually inevitable and can be good when properly approached, we know that it is important to have unity as we work together. Whether we lead or follow, it is important to work together in unity. In Romans 12:18, Paul says, "If possible, so far as it depends on you, be at peace with all men." By God's grace, we can and will unite and be at peace with our colleagues as well as all other people.

CHAPTER SEVEN
THE ROLE OF AUTHORITY
Introduction

The mother of James and John expressed her desire for her sons to have positions of honor at the right hand and left hand of Jesus. Clearly, the other disciples felt that James and John wanted these positions, and they became indignant. It was at this point that Jesus spoke about the Gentiles lording it over others and exercising authority. With this in mind, this chapter is about "The Role of Authority." In our discussion of authority, we include the related concept of power.

What Jesus said presupposes that the leaders of the Gentiles not only had the authority but also the power to rule over their subjects. Thus, the two key words for this chapter are authority and power. As Charles H. Kraft points out, "The Greek words representing what Jesus gave His followers are *dunamis* [δύναμις], power, and *exousia* [ἐξουσία], authority" (1997, 66). He defines power and authority as follows:

> The power of God is ordinarily referred to as *dunamis* as is the power Jesus gives us (Luke 9:1). But earthly power, whether of rulers, of armies or of weather, was also labelled *dunamis.*" . . . *Exousia*, though often referring to power, focuses on the right to use power rather than on the power itself. . . .It is a personal right, either because of status or by delegation, to assert power, whether in legal, political, social or moral ways in the human world or in the spiritual realm." (1997, 67)

The words *power* and *authority* overlap in meaning, but they are not totally synonymous. Power has to do with the ability a leader has to make others do what he wants, to conform to his will. Authority, on the other hand involves the right to act within the designated spheres. It means that the leader has the freedom to act. A leader may have power without authority, or he may have authority without power. Many leaders, like the Gentile leaders that Jesus mentions, have both power and authority.

Whenever people associate with one another, whether in or out of the church, questions of authority and power arise. Our concern here is with the church. Should there be rank, organization, authority, and power exercised in the body of Christ? Or, should all people be equal and autonomous? We are equal at the foot of the cross. Are we equal in our working relationships? Our Matthew story deals with authority and power and can be applied to its exercise in the church.

Once again, I will present the Matthew story as our text. This time we will focus our attention on verse 25. This verse raises the issue of authority. Although it does not fully treat the subject, it gives us the springboard to bring the issue into focus. Another passage of Scripture, Exodus 18:13-26, will be vital for this chapter. I will present this passage later.

20Then the mother of the sons of Zebedee came to Jesus with her sons, bowing down and making a request of Him.

21And He said to her, "What do you wish?"
She said to Him, "Command that in Your kingdom these two sons of mine may sit one on Your right and one on Your left."

22But Jesus answered, "You do not know what you are asking. Are you able to drink the cup that I am about to drink?" They said to Him, "We are able."

23He said to them, "My cup you shall drink; but to sit on My right and on *My* left, this is not Mine to give, but it is for those for whom it has been prepared by My Father."

24And hearing *this*, the ten became indignant with the two brothers.

25But Jesus called them to Himself and said, "You know that the rulers of the Gentiles lord it over them, and *their* great men exercise authority over them.

26It is not this way among you, but whoever wishes to become great among you shall be your servant.

27and whoever wishes to be first among you shall be your slave;

28just as the Son of Man did not come to be served, but to serve, and to give His life a ransom for many."

We will begin this chapter with the concerns of Jesus and talk about the abuse of authority. Then, we will discuss the necessity of authority, the right use of authority, and end with a discussion of what we should do. As explained above, this involves the abuse of power as well.

The Abuse of Authority

As virtually all people would recognize, authority can be abused. Very often this happens when people subscribe to a popular philosophy that makes power the priority of their existence. This approach is self-defeating. As leaders, we should avoid all tyranny. We turn now to a discussion of these matters.

First, Jesus warns the disciples against the abuse of authority and power. He used the Gentiles and their "great men," or leaders, as an example. Jesus said (v. 25): "You know that the rulers of the Gentiles lord it over them, and *their* great men exercise authority over them."

Jesus was not giving a full treatment of authority and power in this verse. Other Scriptures let us know there is a proper use of power in leadership, but power as an end in itself is an abuse. This is what Jesus strikes down. He went on to say (verse 26), "It is not this way among you." He was speaking against power as the indispensable element of leadership. When power is the primary objective, it can soon turn to tyranny. With regard to power, Tead indicates that:

> The desire for enhancement of the essential ego of every individual is one of his central driving motives—one which colors and influences all behavior, and one which is, of course, natural and essential. . . . But this love of self-enhancement can easily get out of hand; and if the leadership situation becomes, as it well may, the sole channel for the release of the will to power, the dangers of excess are real. (1935, 215)

Second, Michael Korda expresses a popular secular philosophy. Although written in 1975, millions of people in the world cling to this as their philosophy of life. According to Korda:

> All of life is a game of power. The object of the game is simple enough: to know what you want and get it. The moves of the game, by contrast, are infinite and complex, although they usually involve the manipulation of people and situations to your advantage. As for the rules, these are only discovered by playing the game to the end.
>
> Some people play the game for money, some for security or fame, others for sex, most for some combination of these objectives. The master players . . . seek power itself, knowing that power can be used to obtain money, sex, security or fame. None of these alone constitutes power; but power can produce them all. (1975, 4)

Christian leaders should not be engaged in the power game. Although they do exercise authority and have to deal with relationships involving power, they should not make power itself their objective. When they do, they seriously endanger their cause. This is precisely what Christ spoke against. Rather than focusing on power, they make service the indispensable factor of their leadership. Their service enhances their co-workers as well as the people that they serve together.

Third, the abuse of power is self-defeating. In Ecclesiastes 8:9, Solomon says (NIV), "There is a time when a man lords it over others to his own hurt." Many leaders have suffered because they have put power above service. In so doing, they have damaged their own leadership and cause.

Apparently, the son of Solomon, Rehoboam, did not pay attention to his father. He sought advice on how to reign (2 Chron. 10:6-19). The old men (verse 7) advised kindness. The young men (verse 10) advised Rehoboam to tell the people, "My little finger is thicker than my father's loins!" Rehoboam should have remembered the words of his father and followed the advice of the old men. Instead, he accepted the counsel of the young men. Verse 19 tells us the result, "So Israel has been in rebellion against the house of David to this day."

Fourth, we must avoid tyranny. Jesus spoke about the "great men" of the Gentiles. He used two Greek words to describe their leadership. These words are *katakurieuousin* (κατακυριεύουσιν), meaning "lord it over," and *katexousiazousin* (κατεξουσιάζουσιν), which is commonly translated "exercise authority." According to Robertson, one possible translation of the second word is "play the tyrant" (1930, 162). The Gentiles mentioned by Jesus were high officials who tyrannized the people they professed to lead. In other words, the essential feature of their leadership was power and authority. As Christian leaders, we must avoid "lording it over" people and "playing the tyrant." While authority must be exercised, it must not be done with power as an end in itself. Paradoxically, such "greatness' is really "weakness."

The Necessity of Authority

Authority is a necessary element in human existence and in our relationship with God. We will begin with comments about the authority that Jesus has and has given to us. Then, we will discuss authority as a part of human association, Biblical examples of the use of authority, and lines of authority that help organizations function properly.

First, according to Matthew 28:18, Jesus said, "All authority has been given to Me in heaven and on earth," and He has passed great measures of that authority on to us as believers. Kraft made a full study of the believer's authority. With regard to Jesus and the disciples, he writes:

> During His ministry, He sent them out to heal and cast out demons in "power and authority" (Luke 9:1; see Luke 10:9, 17). The disciples had worked in Jesus' authority while He was on earth, and He had promised them that when He left, He would send them the Holy Spirit, the One who had empowered Him, to enable them to do all He had done and more (John 14:12). (1997, 39)

Second, Jesus spoke against the abuse of authority, but He did not deny that authority is a part of human association. Authority, submission, and organization are all facts of existence and group life. We cannot live and work together without having leaders and followers. When we have leaders and followers, authority is involved. We can illustrate this with several Biblical examples.

One. Citizens should respect the authority of government. Paul tells us in Romans 13:1: "Every person is to be in subjection to the governing authorities. For there is no authority except from God, and those which exist are established by God." Similarly, Peter writes: "Submit yourselves for the Lord's sake to every human institution, whether to a king as the one in authority, or to governors as sent by him for the punishment of evildoers and the praise of those who do right. For such is the will of God that by doing right you may silence the ignorance of foolish men" (1 Pet. 2:13-15).

Two, With regard to husbands and wives, Paul wrote: "Wives, *be subject* to your own husbands, as to the Lord. For the husband is the head of the wife, as Christ also is the head of the church," He Himself *being* the Savior of the body" (Eph. 5:22-23). Paul balances these words with this further comment: "Husbands, love your wives, just as Christ also loved the church and gave Himself up for her" (Eph. 5:25).

Three. Concerning children and their parents, we read in Ephesians 6:1: "Children, obey your parents in the Lord, for this is right." Once again, Paul brings balance. He states: "Fathers, do not provoke your children to anger, but bring them up in the discipline and instruction of the Lord" (Eph. 6:4).

Four. Peter addresses the role of authority with regard to pastors and their congregations. His comments with regard to the shepherd and the flock suggest the right exercise of authority but also echo the words of Jesus against tyranny. He gives this exhortation (I Pet. 5:2-4):

> [2]shepherd the flock of God among you, exercising oversight not under compulsion, but voluntarily, according to *the will of* God; and not for sordid gain, but with eagerness;
> [3]nor yet as lording it over those allotted to your charge, but proving to be examples to the flock.
> [4]And when the Chief Shepherd appears, you will receive the unfading crown of glory.

Five. Concerning each other, Paul wrote to the Ephesians "and be subject to one another in the fear of Christ" (Eph. 5:21). By exhorting us to be "subject," he also acknowledges that there is authority. Peter makes a similar comment: "You younger men, likewise, be subject to *your* elders; and all of you, clothe yourselves with humility toward one another, for God is opposed to the proud, but gives grace to the humble (1 Pet. 5:5).

The Biblical evidence about authority is tempered with comments about love, tenderness, and the dangers of excess. As Peter knew, authority has its limits. When he was faced with the command not to witness, he declared: "We must obey God rather than men" (Acts 5:29). This dictum applies to all of the relationships mentioned above. Nevertheless, the Biblical data strongly supports the proper role, use, and submission to authority.

Third, when people associate and decide to do things together, management and organization become key factors. Organization, like authority, is supported in the Bible. A key story has to do with Moses judging and leading the people. The story is found in Exodus 18:13-26:

> [13]It came about the next day that Moses sat to judge the people, and the people stood about Moses from the morning until the evening.
> [14]Now when Moses' father-in-law saw all that he was doing for the people, he said, "What is this thing that you are doing for the people?

Why do you alone sit *as judge* and all the people stand about you from morning until evening?"

[15]Moses said to his father-in-law, "Because the people come to me to inquire of God.

[16]When they have a dispute, it comes to me, and I judge between a man and his neighbor and make known the statutes of God and His laws."

[17]Moses' father-in-law said to him, "The thing that you are doing is not good.

[18]You will surely wear out, both yourself and these people who are with you, for the task is too heavy for you; you cannot do it alone.

[19]"Now listen to me: I will give you counsel, and God be with you. You be the people's representative before God, and you bring the disputes to God,

[20]then teach them the statutes and the laws, and make known to them the way in which they are to walk and the work they are to do.

[21]Furthermore, you shall select out of all the people able men who fear God, men of truth, those who hate dishonest gain; and you shall place *these* over them *as* leaders of thousands, of hundreds, of fifties and of tens.

[22]"Let them judge the people at all times; and let it be that every major dispute they will bring to you, but every minor dispute they themselves will judge. So it will be easier for you, and they will bear *the burden* with you.

[23]If you do this thing and God *so* commands you, then you will be able to endure, and all these people also will go to their place in peace."

[24] So Moses listened to his father-in-law and did all that he had said.

[25]Moses chose able men out of all Israel and made them heads over the people, leaders of thousands, of hundreds, of fifties and of tens.

[26]They judged the people at all times; the difficult dispute they would bring to Moses, but every minor dispute they themselves would judge.

This story touches on a whole series of management topics. It is beyond the scope of this book to deal at length with these topics, but I will name some of the topics and comment briefly on them. Like the Matthew story, this Moses story provides a springboard to many subjects.

One. Time with God.—Moses was exhorted by his father-in-law to lead in a new way (verse 19). He was to spend more time with God and bring the disputes of the people to Him. This would give him more rest and clearer vision. This is a good message for all Christian leaders.

Two. Time Management.—Moses needed to manage his time better. He was taking too much time judging the people. The father-in-law of Moses said, "The thing that you are doing is not good. You will surely wear out, both yourself and these people who are with you, for the task is too heavy for you; you cannot do it alone" (verses 17-18). Moses explained to his father-in-law that the people came to him to inquire of God. Because the people came, Moses made known the statutes of God and His laws (verses 15-16).

Three. Delegation.—The father-in-law of Moses advised him to delegate much of his work to others. He was to "teach" others the statutes of the laws and "make known" to them the way in which they were to walk (verses 20-21). Moreover, Moses was to select able men to place them over others" (verse 21).

Four. Structure.—As verses 21 and 24-25 indicate, Moses was to have leaders of thousands, hundreds, fifties, and tens. This suggests that the leaders of tens would report to the leaders of fifties, and the leaders of fifties, to the leaders of hundreds, and so on. In other words, a definite structure was advised. To lead the thousands of people through the wilderness for forty years required some organization.

Five. Job Descriptions.—In verses 20 and 22, a job description was given. With regard to the people, Moses was advised to "teach them the statutes and the laws, and make known to them the way in which they are to walk and the work they are to do" (verse 20). As for the leaders, "Let them judge the people at all times; and let it be that every major dispute they will bring to you, but every minor dispute they themselves will judge. So it will be easier for you, and they will bear *the burden* with you" (verse 22). The leaders were to "judge" the people and help "bear the burden." This burden was very great and could only be handled as it was divided among the leaders.

Six. Standard of Performance.—This Moses story does not specifically present a standard of performance, but we can assume that Moses expected the leaders to be good judges. Because they would judge well, the people, as Moses' father-in-law proposes, "will go to their place in peace" (verse 23). This projected result could be viewed as a standard that the leaders were to achieve.

Seven. Responsibility.—The leaders would be given responsibility. Verse 26 tells us, "every minor dispute they themselves would judge." The leaders of fifties no doubt had more responsibility than the leaders of tens. The scope of their work would be larger. There were limits to their responsibility. The hard cases were still to go to Moses (verse 26).

Eight. Qualifications.—Verse 21 gives us the qualifications for the leaders. "Furthermore, you shall select out of all the people able men who fear God, men of truth, those who hate dishonest gain; and you shall place *these* over them *as* leaders of thousands, of hundreds, of fifties and of tens." Clearly, it was important for the leaders to be men of strong character and ability.

Nine. Training.—The Moses story recognizes the importance of training. The story emphasizes the teaching and training of the people (v. 20). Although the story does not specifically mention training for the leaders, we can assume that Moses taught them how to properly judge. Moreover, they were among the people who did receive teaching and training.

Ten. Service.—Moses' father-in-law advised Moses to delegate some of his work (verses 18-20). This suggests that the interests of the people, as well as the health of Moses, were in full view. The people would be better served through good oversight and management. Moses would be a better leader, and the people would have more ready access to help. The selected leaders would have the well-being of the people at heart.

The Right Use of Authority

Given that authority and power are necessary, we must consider the right use of these elements in leadership. Leaders should not want authority for its own sake, but rather as a tool to accomplish mutually accepted objectives for the people. Several points follow from this.

First, authority is properly used when it focuses on service rendered to people. We organize in order to serve others, not to rule over them. Using the words of Jesus as a model (Mark 2:27), we might say that "management is made for man and not man for management." In the Matthew story Christ was speaking to men who wanted positions of honor and power. Let them pay the price and desire, first of all, to serve. Then, if they rise to positions of authority, they will use the authority correctly.

Second, ultimately, the power of individual leaders and organizations rests on service. Although power can be maintained in nations by military might, the stronger basis for authority is service. Even authority maintained by armies will crumble if it is too oppressive. Thus, the thoughts of the Christian leader ought always to turn to what serves the best interests of the people he leads. The leader who does this will command the respect and admiration of the people.

Third, some leaders are concerned mainly with their authority. They are the ones who will say "You are under me." This stands in contrast to the leaders who put the priority on the development of staff members. Also, the effective executive is one who stresses his or her contribution to group goals. Peter Drucker makes this insightful comment:

> The man who focuses on efforts and who stresses his downward authority is a subordinate no matter how exalted his title and rank. But the man who focuses on contribution and who takes responsibility for results no matter how junior, is, in the most literal sense of the phrase, "top management." He holds himself accountable of the whole. (1985, 55)

Our Actions

Major volumes have been written about how to be a servant leader. Here, I will mention just a few points that may be helpful. I will deal more extensively with this subject in chapters nine, ten and twelve.

First, we must learn both to lead and to follow. Both leading and following can be done with poor motivation or with proper attitudes. Every leader is also a follower in some situations. Although every follower is not a leader in the sense of having a high position, he or she can lead in service. It is important for us to learn the etiquette of both leadership and followership roles. Whether leader or follower, we should approach each situation with humility. This does not prevent us from being creative in leading and following.

Second, we should lead with diligence. In Romans 12:6-8, Paul writes about the gifts of the Spirit. He declares: "Since we have gifts that differ according to the grace given to us, each of us is to exercise them accordingly" (verse 6). Among the gifts, he lists leadership. In verse 8, we read, "he who leads, [lead] with diligence." We must not take the gift of leadership lightly. When God has bestowed this gift, we should exercise it. We need not claim we have it! Others will know whether we do or not. When we do, we must take responsibility, put our hearts into service, and follow the Lord where He leads.

Third, we should esteem others highly, including both our co-workers and our leaders. The ideal action for all of us is to respect all others at whatever level they work in our organizations. We all know people who are compliant to those above them on the organization chart and disrespectful to those beneath. On the other hand, there are people who are respectful to peers but disrespectful to those above. It is better to respect all people, wherever they are on the organization chart.

When we talk about people with whom we associate, many people focus on their superiors, not the people they lead. At any level of activity, this is true! Some chafing would appear to be normal. After all, our superiors can impede or speed our progress, and sometimes they do both. Nevertheless, good followers will usually find ways to get along with superiors.

With regard to esteeming our leaders, Paul says: "But we request of you, brethren, that you appreciate those who diligently labor among you, and have charge over you in the Lord and give you instruction, that you esteem them very highly in love because of their work. Live in peace with one another" (1 Thess. 5:12-13). As our leaders serve, it is important that we esteem them for their service.

Fourth, we should meet needs and avoid all abuse of power. We must not do things just to maintain power, but to serve others. The needs of people cry out to be met. Eventually, these needs will override all other concerns. There are occasions in the life of every leader when authority has to be exercised, but it should be done with the right motive. When a leader is meeting needs, he or she does not have to use power nearly as often. There are many felt needs that cry out to be met. Each of these needs is an opportunity for the leader to build a strong team. There are, of course, felt needs that simply cannot be met by the leader. So the leadership task becomes one of keeping people on board even though those needs are not met.

Conclusion

Once again we see that service is the indispensable element of Christian leadership. All else is subordinate to this. When we have this principle clearly in view, it will guide us in all that we do. We will exercise authority when it is our responsibility to do so, but with the well-being of our staff and our constituency in mind. The ideal of service will move us to act in ways that are for the common good.

Our leadership will involve us in the organizational life of those we lead. The Moses story is a springboard to a consideration of many management principles and practices. Management is not antithetical to servant leadership. Rather, when done properly, it provides a way to achieve the common good.

We must all remember that Christ is Lord! Because He is Lord, we must subordinate all that we are and do to Him. All of us, as leaders subordinate to Him, must seek His will and simply implement His commands. When followers, as well as leaders, have sought the will of God and have a common understanding of that will, great unity and sense of purpose prevails.

CHAPTER EIGHT

HAZARDS OF LEADERSHIP

Introduction

The indispensable element of servant leadership and servant greatness is service. We think of service in terms of meeting needs, helping the group achieve common goals, and enhancing the lives of the group. The group has come to find these goals desirable. Although leaders may have a clear understanding of their role, they must also realize that there are pitfalls to leadership.

All leaders, including servant leaders, are confronted with hazards to their leadership. Unfortunately, all too many leaders succumb to the pitfalls that they face. Our text, the Matthew story, makes known several hazards and sparks our thinking about others. The Matthew story states:

[20]Then the mother of the sons of Zebedee came to Jesus with her sons, bowing down and making a request of Him.

[21]And He said to her, "What do you wish?"

She said to Him, "Command that in Your kingdom these two sons of mine may sit one on Your right and one on Your left."

[22]But Jesus answered, "You do not know what you are asking. Are you able to drink the cup that I am about to drink?" They said to Him, "We are able."

[23]He said to them, "My cup you shall drink; but to sit on My right and on *My* left, this is not Mine to give, but it is for those for whom it has been prepared by My Father."

[24]And hearing *this*, the ten became indignant with the two brothers.

[25]But Jesus called them to Himself and said, "You know that the rulers of the Gentiles lord it over them, and *their* great men exercise authority over them.

[26]It is not this way among you, but whoever wishes to become great among you shall be your servant.

[27]and whoever wishes to be first among you shall be your slave;

[28]just as the Son of Man did not come to be served, but to serve, and to give His life a ransom for many."

James and John clearly wanted to have positions of honor and power. This motivation, if not kept subordinate to service objectives, can be a hazard for leaders. Clearly, James and John were out of line and did not understand the cost of leadership. The indignation of the other ten disciples suggests that they were jealous and envious. No doubt they, too, wanted places of honor and power. Many leaders fall prey to this hazard.

The comments Jesus made reveal that the disciples needed to be instructed about the abuse of power. A very real hazard is to misuse the power and authority that Christ has given to us. Leaders may want to exercise raw power to gain their objectives. Jesus spoke against this and pointed the disciples to service as the way to lead.

In this chapter, we will consider two other hazards to leadership—compromise and manipulation. Jesus does not deal directly with these hazards in this story, but leaders commonly are confronted with them. When leaders are guided primarily by the motive of power, they are strongly tempted to manipulate others and to compromise in the wrong way. The prospective leader needs to be aware of these hazards.

Compromise

The goal of Christian leaders is to serve the people they lead. As they attempt to meet this goal, they will be faced with the issue of compromise. People have different views on a wide range of subjects. To the extent that those views affect the direction of the group's activities, the need for compromise may arise.

First, compromise can be either bad or good. When we speak of compromise, we normally mean coming to an agreement by making mutual concessions. Each side gives up something in order to come to agreement. As long as each side is not giving up ethical principles, compromise can be good. When wrong concessions are made, then it is bad. Obviously, there is often a lot of disagreement about what should be given up and what should not.

Second, people in all walks of life face the issue of compromise. Let us consider, as examples, salesmen, politicians, and church leaders. We readily recognize that salesmen and politicians might face compromise, but are not so quick to recognize this in the church.

One. A maxim of sales work is "Find out what people want and help them get it." Another way of saying this is, "Find out what the needs of the people are and devise some way to meet them." Much marketing theory is built on these premises. Normally, people will not purchase what they do not want or need. Thus, selling people what they want instead of what we want for them is usually a wise compromise!

However, we should not thoughtlessly heed these exhortations. Many times people want what is not good for them and even those things which endanger them. Moreover, people frequently put "felt needs" above "real needs." The Christian leader is obligated to act in the "best interest" of the people. To do otherwise would be to compromise his principles and integrity. When this happens, we become "compromisers" in a negative sense.

Two. Political life is filled with compromise. Indeed, without compromise, few laws would make it through national legislative bodies. Before votes are taken, much negotiation goes on behind the scenes. Strong drives are made to gather the votes for or against an issue. Some compromise is essential, moral, and legitimate, but on some issues, strong stands must be taken.

John F. Kennedy's book, *Profiles in Courage*, is a tribute to men and women who did not compromise with regard to their convictions. They would not "sell out." When politicians take a courageous stand, putting national interest above personal interest, we usually call them "statesmen." Many things have to be considered when a politician decides on what issues to compromise and on what issues to stand firm. Above all, politicians, like all others, need to maintain high ethical standards.

Three. In the church, similar situations arise. Many issues arise in board meetings which require discussion, consensus, give-and-take, sometimes concessions, and in a word—compromise. Much of the time, this is a normal, creative, and acceptable process.

Unfortunately, church leaders, including lay leaders and ministers, are sometimes tempted to compromise in a negative sense. When church attendance is low, leaders may be tempted to forsake their basic principles in order to attract people. People raising funds may be tempted to forsake their principles of integrity in other to gather the funds. We happily recognize, however, that nearly all church leaders remain faithful and do not yield to these temptations.

Third, very often leaders are confronted with a dilemma. Leaders who firmly stand for their convictions against the will of the people they lead are usually accused of being dictators. If they sense the will of the people and do it, they may be said to be weak and may be called compromisers.

Between these poles, every elected leader lives, moves, and has his being. Ideally, every leader would stand fully and uncompromisingly for his essential, vital, and moral convictions. The leader would compromise only on non-essentials or matters that are not of moral importance. When the leader's convictions match the convictions of the people he serves, the leadership task is not as difficult.

As leaders, we must know when to yield and when to stand. Normally, we must stand on issues that will benefit other individuals and the group as a whole and yield on issues that will benefit only yourself. Leadership that is selfish will not long endure. Moreover, we must aim more at helping people achieve their objectives than at control. Some control is necessary, but this control should enhance the group. As much as possible, we should allow freedom within broad guidelines.

Because two people do not usually think alike on all issues, they are probably going to meet situations where compromise is necessary. Each leader must decide where to take a stand and where to yield. A leader who yields on everything, and changes with the wind, lacks moral force. On the other hand, a leader who will yield on nothing overvalues his opinion and will disrupt the harmony of the group.

Fourth, negotiation is the process by which compromises are reached. Many years ago, along with a colleague, I attended a Henry Calero seminar in Holland on negotiation. Calero had videotaped 2,000 negotiations as they happened and had made exhaustive studies of the process. He taught that the emphasis of negotiation should be on "win-win" rather than "win-lose." If at all possible, everyone should come out of the negotiation a winner. Very often, this involves compromise.

Calero said that the 19th century man stressed confrontation. This frequently led to war and the desire to fight to the finish. Mainly because of nuclear power, man in the last part of the 20th century put more emphasis on compromise. When both sides have nuclear power, war is not a viable option. This means that nations have to enter into negotiations to avoid war and settle their problems. Although the view of Calero was true to a degree, the "win-lose" approach was still around when nuclear war was not an issue.

Now, in the 21st century, we are faced with a new kind of war—terrorism. To some degree, we have returned to a "win-lose" approach. The reason is clear. The terrorists are willing to die as deliberate suicide victims and believe they have the upper hand in causing pain to their enemies. They are not willing to compromise. When survival is not possible through compromise, survival will have the highest priority.

Fifth, as Christian leaders, what should our approach be? Much depends on the issue which is being discussed. There are times when reaching a compromise is the best approach, but there are times when we should not compromise. Let's look at some of the options.

One. Paul wrote in Romans 12:18, "If possible, so far as it depends on you, be at peace with all men." On some matters, where integrity and moral principle are not involved, we need not take a strong stand. However, compromise may be necessary on non-essentials. It reduces friction, helps us adapt to circumstances, and assists us in getting along with all people. The nature of the issue at stake is of utmost importance.

Two. Christian leaders must avoid the hazard of compromise in a wrong sense. Writing about compromise that is wrong, Sanders declares:

> Compromise is the partial waiving of principle for the sake of reaching agreement. It is always a backward step when we consent to lower our standards, and all too often this is involved in arriving at a compromise. It nearly always involves a scaling down of standards.
>
> The epic contest of Moses with Pharaoh affords a classic example of the progressive temptation to compromise. When Pharaoh discerned Moses' inflexible purpose to take Israel out of Egypt to worship Jehovah, he used all his wiles to frustrate him. (1967, 120)

In spite of the repeated attempts by Pharaoh to get Moses to compromise, Moses refused to give in to temptation. He stayed true to his mission. As a result, he led the children of Israel in their historic departure from Egypt and their crossing of the Red Sea.

It is not only leaders who are confronted with comprise; the entire body of Christ faces this temptation. The trend often arises to so fully adapt to the culture and the environment that there is little difference between the way that Christians live and the living habits of the people at large. In addition, the message of the church may depart from the truth. It is all right to adapt to culture unless true Biblical principles and truth are abandoned. When they are abandoned, the church joins the world in its ways rather than following Christ.

Three. Jesus is our highest example. When He taught, He spoke the truth without compromise. The scribes and chief priests knew this, but they tried to use it against him. When they questioned Jesus, they said to Him, "Teacher, we know that You speak and teach correctly, and You are not partial to any, but teach the way of God in truth" (Luke 20:21). They were trying to trick Him into answering the next question (Luke 20:22), "Is it lawful for us to pay taxes to Caesar, or not?" Jesus avoided their trap by answering, "Then render to Caesar the things that are Caesar's and to God the things that are God's" (Luke 20:25). Even though the scribes and the chief priests were being deceptive, they spoke the truth about Jesus—He spoke and taught correctly. He did not compromise in His teaching of the truth.

Manipulation

Another hazard for leaders is manipulation. Like compromise, the term *manipulation* can be used in both a good and a bad sense. When used of human relationships, the connotation is usually negative. The Christian leader must avoid manipulation in a negative sense.

First, the word *manipulate*, in a good sense, can mean "to treat or operate with the hands or by mechanical means especially in a skilled manner." However, when this term is used in a figurative way, it often takes on negative connotations. In a negative sense, manipulation means "to control or play upon by artful, unfair, or insidious means especially to one's own advantage." Similarly, manipulation means "to change by artful or unfair means so as to serve one's purpose." (Definitions by *Merriam-Webster*)

When a leader is manipulating, he may appear to be serving the interests of the group but is actually serving his own interests. When this is discovered, it is self-defeating. Although the group may initially be for you, they will turn against you. When the group is uncertain, they will live with a certain uneasiness about you as a leader. When people feel manipulated, they will resent the manipulator.

Second, we can illustrate manipulation with some life situations. All of us, probably, have either been manipulated or have engaged in manipulation, and perhaps both, at points in our lives. We are all guilty! Thus, we do not enter this discussion unaware.

One. A well-known book by Dale Carnegie is titled *How to Win Friends and Influence People* (1936). Whatever the contents of the book, the title sounds somewhat manipulative. You have the impression that we are to win friends in order to gain influence. To a degree, we do not find fault with this because winning friends and gaining influence are a part of all social life. Both we who are being won and we who win others know this and do not object. When taken too far, and wrong motives are hidden, then the winning for the sake of influence goes too far. It becomes a hazard.

Two. There is an old baseball story that illustrates manipulation. The idea could just as easily apply to soccer, cricket, or some other sport. The story goes like this (Bits & Pieces, April 30, 1992):

> *In the heyday of the New York Yankees, manager Joe McCarthy once interviewed a coach being brought up to the majors from a Yankee farm team.*
>
> *"How much do you know about psychology?" McCarthy asked.*
>
> *The coach said he had studied it in college.*
>
> *"So you think you're good," said McCarthy.*
>
> *The coach replied "I don't know how good I am, but it's a subject I've studied."*
>
> *"All right," McCarthy said, "I'll give you a test."*
>
> *McCarthy said that a few years before he'd had a problem and had gone to Frankie Crosetti, his shortstop.*
>
> *"Frank," McCarthy said, "I'm not satisfied with the way Lou Gehrig is playing first base. He's too lackadaisical. I want you to help me. From now on, charge every ground ball. When you get it, fire it as quickly and as hard as you can to first base. Knock Gehrig off the bag if you can. I don't care if you throw wild or not, but throw it fast and make it tough for him."*
>
> *Crosetti demurred and said, "Maybe Lou won't like the idea."*
>
> *"Who cares what Gehrig likes?" McCarthy snapped. "Just do as I tell you."*

> *McCarthy then said to the coach, "Now that's the story. What conclusions do you draw from it?"*
>
> *The coach considered the matter for a minute, then answered, "I guess you were trying to wake up Gehrig."*
>
> *"See?" McCarthy shrugged his shoulders in resignation. "You missed the point entirely. There wasn't a thing wrong with Gehrig. Crosetti was the one who was sleeping. I want to wake up Crosetti."*

McCarthy was using the term psychology in the popular sense of manipulation, not the academic sense of the discipline of psychology. Obviously, he knew how to use manipulation in his coaching. What he did was not necessarily bad. No ethical principle was at stake.

Third, In his book entitled *Man, the Manipulator*, Everett L. Shostrom contrasts manipulative behavior with actualizing behavior (1967, 23-24). According to him, manipulators are deceptive, are unaware of real values, emphasize control, and are cynical. By way of contrast, actualizers are honest, fully aware of true values and the interests of others, emphasize freedom and spontaneity, and have a deep trust in themselves and others.

Shostrom's book is filled with examples of manipulation. For example, he describes how parents sometimes manipulate their teen-age sons and daughters. One of these ways is to use illness. A parent may say, "If you don't stop that, I'll have a heart attack." When this is not true, it is manipulation! Similarly, he describes how teen-agers manipulate their parents with illness. When asked to do something, a teen-ager may say, "All right, but I'll probably get sick."

When writing about manipulation in business, Shostrom says, "A businessman who thinks of people only as customers or accounts or clients cannot help, to some degree, regarding these persons as things" (1967, 135). In our culture (USA), almost all businesses speak about their desire to serve our needs. Their advertising is filled with this kind of language, but sometimes the rhetoric is far ahead of the reality. Just shop in their stores, and you will discover this. Paradoxically, when businesses do really care, they prosper because of it.

Both leaders and followers can be manipulative. With regard to followers, some middle managers try to manipulate the top management. They will be too eager to help or obey someone important. We have all been around obsequious people, and they make us uncomfortable. They not only make people around them uncomfortable, they make their leaders feel some discomfort as well.

If all this is true for business, it is even more true in the church. A church leader may regard the people as things who support the church rather than as individuals whose needs he serves. When this news is "out," the attendance may decline. As Christian leaders, we must know that the paradox of service applies to us as well. The more we genuinely serve, the stronger will be our leadership. We must stay close to Christ and let His love for the people guide our lives. The same thing is true for the members of the congregation.

Fourth, many politicians are highly skilled in manipulation. Titus writes: "The politician believes that worthwhile objectives can be realized through the exploitation of the less capable by means of the proper uses of assumptions, impelling motives, and political methods manipulated by the most skilful" (1950). No doubt, some politicians try to avoid manipulation, but it does seem that there is a special temptation in political life to exercise this approach.

Do we have politics in the church? As with many words, the term *politics* can have a good meaning as well as bad. Clearly, we do have political life in the church. When the term is used in its good sense, politics are essential in the conduct of business. For example, we have agendas, resolutions, discussions, and elections. However, we should avoid politics in the negative sense. Unfortunately, this kind of politics sometimes creeps in as well. Because of this, manipulation sometimes can be found in the business life of the church.

Fifth, the real key to being of service is honesty. Let us not promise our colleagues more than we can deliver. We can, and should, develop a greater interest in others and their welfare. However, let us not profess a deep interest we do not have in order to gain something ourselves.

Although some discussion can be stirred up over the normal polite exchanges of everyday life, these exchanges are not excluded by being honest. When we are asked, "How are you?" we can say, "Fine," without worrying about being dishonest. There are many degrees of being fine. If someone really wants to know how we are, we can go further in our reply. These exchanges vary somewhat from culture to culture. What is nearly universal is our desire to have an open and honest relationship with our friends in matters that really count.

The Psalmist wrote these words about a person we might call a manipulator, "His speech was smoother than butter, But his heart was war; His words were softer than oil, Yet they were drawn swords" (Ps. 55:21). Similarly, Proverbs 29:5 says, "A man who flatters his neighbor Is spreading a net for his steps." Underlying these forms of manipulation is a lack of honesty. Anything can be said to achieve one's purpose.

Contrast this with Jesus. Christ both upheld guilelessness in others and lived without deceit in His own life. Speaking of Nathanael, Jesus said, "Behold, an Israelite indeed, in whom is no deceit" (John 1:47). In 1 Peter 2:22, the apostle declared Jesus to be the One "who committed no sin, nor was any deceit found in His mouth."

Guilelessness is a quality to be admired in all Christians and especially in leaders. In Psalm 32:2, we read, "How blessed in the man to whom the Lord does not impute iniquity, And in whose spirit there is no deceit!" Peter cites Psalm 34:12-13 with these words, "The one who desires life, to love and see good days, Must keep his tongue from evil and his lips from speaking deceit" (1 Pet. 3:10). Clearly, the Christian leader should seek to be without guile in serving the people.

Conclusion

The Christian leader is committed to Biblical standards. This sets a high goal for him or her. As a result, the leader must be constantly vigilant to hold up the Biblical teachings in leadership as well as in life. Even the apostle Paul had to stay on guard to avoid the hazards to his ministry. Using a sports analogy, he made this declaration (1 Cor. 9:26-27):

> [26]Therefore I run in such a way, as not without aim; I box in such a way, as not beating the air;
> [27]but I discipline my body and make it my slave, so that, after I have preached to others, I myself will not be disqualified.

Our goal is to serve the best interests of the people we lead. Two of the hazards servant leaders face, including Christian leaders, are the wrong use of manipulation and compromise. The Christian leader must do everything possible to avoid these hazards. Because of our humanity, we do not always live up to the ideal. We must, however, be guided by the ideal and call upon the Lord to help us. Jesus Christ is our highest example. As leaders, let us seek to conform to His manner in leading! He will help us in all things.

CHAPTER NINE

LEADING THROUGH SERVICE

Introduction

All of the chapters in this book have been based on the leadership story in Matthew 20:20-28. Each chapter has highlighted various aspects of the Matthew story. This chapter will focus our attention on verses 26-27. These two verses give the central message of the story which is "Leading through Service." Once again, we will present the entire text.

> ²⁰Then the mother of the sons of Zebedee came to Jesus with her sons, bowing down and making a request of Him.
>
> ²¹And He said to her, "What do you wish?"
> She said to Him, "Command that in Your kingdom these two sons of mine may sit one on Your right and one on Your left."
>
> ²²But Jesus answered, "You do not know what you are asking. Are you able to drink the cup that I am about to drink?" They said to Him, "We are able."
>
> ²³He said to them, "My cup you shall drink; but to sit on My right and on *My* left, this is not Mine to give, but it is for those for whom it has been prepared by My Father."
>
> ²⁴And hearing *this*, the ten became indignant with the two brothers.
>
> ²⁵But Jesus called them to Himself and said, "You know that the rulers of the Gentiles lord it over them, and *their* great men exercise authority over them.
>
> ²⁶It is not this way among you, but whoever wishes to become great among you shall be your servant.
>
> ²⁷and whoever wishes to be first among you shall be your slave;
>
> ²⁸just as the Son of Man did not come to be served, but to serve, and to give His life a ransom for many."

Jesus addressed His remarks in verses 26-27 to "whoever wishes to become great among you" and "whoever wishes to be first among you." As Lenski points out, the human will is involved. The same Greek verb θέλω (*thelō*) is used in both Matthew 20:26, 27 and the parallel passage in Mark 9:35. Commenting on Mark 9:35, Lenski writes:

It is a question of the will: εἴ τις θέλει (*ei tis thelei* [if anyone desires]), one must determine, set his will upon being first [or great]. The thing does not drop into one's lap, it requires will, effort. But this thing of being first is open to anyone τις (*tis*); we may all be first. In the world all cannot possibly be first. This indefinite pronoun is an invitation to you and to me to be first just as it invited the Twelve to step into first place. (1946, 391, Transliteration Mine.)

To those who have the desire to be great, to be first, or to be great leaders, Jesus points the way. The way, as we soon will see, is paradoxical and very challenging and costly.

Before we proceed to discuss leading through service, we need to see the relationship between greatness, being first, and leadership. James and John wanted positions of honor and power, greatness in this sense. Jesus replied with His declaration that true greatness and being first is achieved through service. Although one may be great in serving without leading a group, the emphasis of the story is on those who do. Jesus does not use the word "leader," but He clearly is talking mainly about those who guide and direct a group.

When Jesus gives His reply, we see Him as the Master Teacher at work. In short, pithy, and profound statements, he challenges His disciples both to great achievement and to the right kind of motivation and accomplishment. As we study His teaching, we will discuss (1) the types of leaders, (2) an inverted order of greatness, (3) the necessity of meeting needs, and (4) ways to lead by serving.

Types of Leaders

The term "leader" can be used in a variety of ways. In chapter one, we identified several types of leaders. Here, we will recall those types in order to identify the ones that Jesus has in mind in verses 26-27.

First, many people are leaders in the sense that they are explorers. They are the first ones to climb the mountains or to discover some new territory or to try out new methods. As we said in chapter one, they are "*ahead*" of the group. They are sometimes in a very lonely position. The very nature of their task demands this.

Tead draws a contrast between the guides and the explorers in mountain climbing with these comments: "They [the explorers] are, no doubt, the greater climbers; they may be compared to the seers and prophets of the world. The world needs both kinds. But the opportunity for the guide type of leader in a democracy is particularly great" (1935, 269).

Second, James and John were not trying to be explorers. They wanted to be great and first among the disciples. It appears that they wanted to have positions of honor and to rule over others. Thus they wanted to be either "*a head*" or "*the head*" of the group. We might think of "*a head*" as a guide and "*the head*" as being more autocratic.

The guides help others climb the mountains. They are coaches, counselors, teachers, and are people-centered. They help people cooperate toward the goals which they come to find very desirable. There is self-sacrifice in this which the "explorer" is sometimes loathe to make.

Third, Jesus was a prophet, priest, and king. The teaching of Jesus in verses 26-27 applies in some way to all three types of leaders. The prophet is "*ahead*" of the group. Even so, his prophetic activity and pronouncements should serve the group. The king is "*the head*" of the group. Typically, kings tend to be dictatorial, but they will experience true greatness only through service. The priest is "*a head*" of the group. He serves as a guide. He is at his best when he serves the interests of the group. In all three cases, the premise is that serving is the strongest way to lead, but the main emphasis is on those who want to be "*a head*" or "*the head*" of a group.

An Inverted Order

What Jesus says about being great and being first stands in contrast to what much of the world believes. However, even secular business and other organizations have come to see that it is best to lead through service. The term "servant leader" has become very popular. Several points can be made.

First, a popular idea of greatness is completely inverted by Christ. Many people think of greatness in terms of rulers who have authority and power. Jesus declared that true greatness comes through service. Greatness, as defined by Jesus, transcends authority. The leader may have authority and power, but the indispensable element is service. The great leader is the servant of those whom he leads. As Robertson writes: "This is a complete reversal of popular opinion then and now" (1930, 162).

Through the use of two triangles, we can contrast the ruler and his authority with the servant leader. To illustrate the ruler, draw a triangle with one angle, the apex, at the top. Then put the ruler, the person regarded as great, on the apex and the people being led below. The bottom horizontal line represents the people. Jesus turns the triangle upside down. To illustrate His approach to the servant leader, draw an inverted triangle with the single angle at the bottom. Then put the servant, the truly great person, on this angle and the people above. The horizontal line, which is now at the top, signifies the people being served.

Second, the inverted triangle raises this question: "What does Jesus mean by the terms *servant* and *slave*?" To answer this, we will examine the way in which Jesus used them, and what that means for us. Jesus used these terms in a special paradoxical sense. A paradox reconciles positions that at first glance seem to be contradictory. To many people, the terms *leader* and *servant* describe totally different spheres. Jesus reconciles these terms by declaring that we can lead and be great by serving. Moreover, He lets us know that we can step up by stepping down! If we want to be first, we must step down from servant to slave.

One. Whoever would be great must be the servant. The word servant is a translation of the Greek word *diakonos* (διάκονος). According to Lenski, "A διάκονος [*diakonos*] is one who is intent on the service he is rendering to others. Thus greatness in the kingdom is measured by the readiness and the amount of blessed service rendered to Christ's people" (1943, 791, Transliteration mine). Obviously, one can be "ahead" in service without leading a group, but the main point Jesus makes is that one must serve to be great as "a head" or "the head" of a group.

Two. The person who wishes to climb a step up from greatness to being first must step down! The word "slave" is a translation of the Greek word *doulos* (δοῦλος). The *doulos* is the lowest of all servants. This word is sometimes translated as "bond-servant." The *doulos* has a degree of commitment beyond the *diakonos* to meeting the needs of the people he or she serves. The leader who would be first must make the greater commitment to service.

Third, servants and especially slaves are under the orders of their masters. With respect to Christ, the answer is clear. We are to be completely under His orders at all times and willing to do His bidding. The apostle Paul opened his epistle to the Romans with these words: "Paul, a bond-servant [*doulos*] of Christ Jesus, called *as* an apostle, set apart for the gospel of God" (Rom. 1:1). Paul was fully committed to Christ and the preaching of the gospel.

Given our submission to Christ, leaders may still ask, "In what sense are we to be the servants and slaves of the people we lead?" With regard to them, the work agreement between the leader and the group defines the relationship. For example, a pastor may have a defined working relationship with the board which includes matters of authority. However, we are speaking of something which is deeper than this. We are speaking about what we must do to meet the needs of the people.

Are leaders under obligation to the wants and frivolous desires of the people we lead? Our example is Christ. He did not do everything people wanted. Rather, He did what was in their best interest. I believe this is our obligation. We are servants and slaves of the best interests of those we serve. At times, this requires some serious and profound thought. We do not have the strength, time, energy, or obligation to be on-call for every frivolous demand. We do have an obligation to serve people in such a way that their long-term and highest needs are met.

Fourth, the apostle Paul and Jesus provide the examples of service that will guide us in our activities. Both of them were totally committed to meeting the needs of the people, yet were not servants and slaves in the sense of being under the command of the people in all things.

One. Paul both declares his freedom and his willingness to serve others. He writes, "For though I am free from all men, I have made myself a slave to all, that I might win the more" (1 Cor. 9:19). Paul is willing to make any adaptation to people under the Law and people not under the Law in order to win others to Christ. He would not, of course, go so far as to compromise the gospel. Moreover, the choice as to which needs to meet is still his.

Two. We draw the same conclusion with regard to Jesus. He fully served, but was not under the control of the people. He remained, always, the Savior of the world. As such, He could not compromise with the world. Wolff is on point with the following comments:

> Jesus came to serve. He was the servant of the Lord par excellence. His service was motivated by love and culminated in death. He served to the point of giving his life. At the same time, he never allowed people to use him for selfish purposes. He never confirmed them in their egotism through his service. His service

did not promote the pride of man. The purpose of his service was redemptive, to free man from selfishness and sin as dominating principles. (1970, 31-32)

Meeting Needs

Meeting needs is a very large subject. Our entire national economy thrives when people have jobs and are busy meeting needs. The same principle applies to the church. When the church meets needs, it grows. I have selected several points about meeting needs for discussion here.

First, the fundamental principle in leadership is that people are served as their best and real needs are met. These needs are many and varied. Pastors and churches must focus their attention on needs and determine how to meet them. As needs are met, attendance and the impact of the churches will grow. If needs are not met, the influence of the churches will diminish.

There are many functions that a leader must perform in order for the needs of the people to be met. A leader cannot leave these tasks undone or the group will descend into chaos. James C. Hunter amplifies this concept as follows:

> Servant leadership does not allow one to abdicate his or her leadership responsibility to define the mission, set the rules governing behavior, set standards, and define accountability. The servant leader does not commission a poll, conduct a committee meeting or have a democratic vote to determine the answers to these questions. Indeed, people look to the leader to provide this direction.
>
> However, once this direction has been provided, it becomes time to turn the organization structure upside down and help people win! The leadership now becomes responsive to those being led by identifying and meeting their legitimate needs so they can become the best they are capable of becoming and effectively accomplish the stated missions. (2004, 9)

Second, various needs are emphasized by psychologists. William Glasser, for example, stresses two basic needs: "the need to love and be loved and the need to feel that we are worthwhile to ourselves and others" (1965, 9). When we stop to think about it, we realize how important these two needs are. People must find responsible ways to meet both these needs.

We as Christian leaders can point people to God who loves them and whom they ought to love and who puts the highest value on them. God so values people that He gave His Son to die for them. Moreover, we can develop our Christian community in these virtues, into caring and esteeming societies. These characteristics will strengthen the bonds of the people with the rest of the body of Christ.

Another well-known psychologist, A. H. Maslow, dealt extensively with human needs. In 1943, he presented a five-stage model of basic human needs that included the following: (1) physiological, (2) safety, (3) love and belonging, (4) esteem, and (5) self-actualization (1943). Later, according to Sam McLeod, Maslow added cognitive and aesthetic needs; following this he added a category of transcendence needs (2014, simplypsychology.org).

The needs normally are listed from lower to higher. McLeod, for example, presents Maslow's eight stages of needs in the following order: (1) physiological, (2) safety, (3) love and belonging, (4) esteem, (5) cognitive, (6) aesthetic, (7) self-actualization, and (8) transcendence (2014, simplypsychology.org). Fulfilment in the first six stages contributes to self-actualization.

Mark E. Koltko-Rivera uses the term "self-transcendence" in place of the word transcendence. He points out that this stage has not always been recognized as a part of Maslow's hierarchy. However, he holds that Maslow "amended his model, placing self-transcendence as a motivational step beyond self-actualization" (2006, 302). He further states that "At the level of self-transcendence, the individual's own needs are put aside, to a great extent, in favor of service to others and to some higher force or cause conceived as being outside the personal self" (2006, 306-307).

It is generally recognized: (1) that the lower needs normally are satisfied before the higher ones, (2) that all needs are just partially satisfied, (3) that the higher needs are more unsatisfied, (4) that sometimes the higher needs are satisfied before the lower needs, and (5) that there are exceptions to these positions.

Jesus was concerned about all the human needs of all people. We see Him, for example, meeting physiological needs by healing the sick. However, His primary emphasis was on the spiritual needs of the people. With regard to obtaining clothing, food, and something to drink, Jesus admonished, "But seek first His kingdom and His righteousness, and all these things will be added to you" (Matt. 6:33). This principle applies, I believe, to all of our needs.

Third, one of man's needs is to be unselfish. Unless we acknowledge this, we can become cynical. The cynical person does not believe in any genuine expressions of altruism. Such a view is hopelessly pessimistic. We understand that people can be selfish and that, at best, they normally act altruistically only some of the time, but those moments are to be prized, encouraged, and honored.

Many church people give generously. They give for a lot of reasons. Very often, people give to a need with which they identify. Some of the reasons are selfish, but we must remember that meeting the needs of others is the long-term, sustaining reason. Giving to the church, donations to missions, and meeting local needs all depend on this. Our highest example is Christ who gave everything, including His life, for us.

Fourth, leadership cannot be sustained without force unless needs are being met. When we are meeting needs, our leadership will be stronger. We will be stronger when (1) all the needs of people are met, (2) the needs of more people are met, and (3) needs are met in greater depth. Also, our leadership will endure longer when the best interests, not the short-term interests, of the people are met. If we only meet superficial needs, the people will soon depart from us.

Ways to Lead Through Service

As we seek to meet the needs of the people we lead, we look for practical ways to produce the desired results. There are many ways to lead through service. We will turn now to a discussion of several of these ways.

First, one way to lead through service is to help others find the will of God. This is largely a matter of helping them find themselves—their talents, their ideals, and their ministries. The Spirit distributes ministry gifts, but He usually acts in harmony with natural talents. Within limits, God wants all people to actualize all their potential. Helping people find self-fulfillment within the will of God is a legitimate way to serve them.

After years of working in administration with people, I have reached the following conclusion. Although there are exceptions, most people (including ministers) will decide to occupy the role which most enhances their ministry. They will usually stay in a given role only as long as it does. This is not contradictory to the thought that most believers would do the will of God even if it did not enhance their ministries. However, sometimes people believe that the will of God for them is what blesses the things they are doing for Him.

Second, a related point is that we serve people when we help them achieve great things. According to *Bits and Pieces*, a good example of helping others become achievers is Charles Percy (April, 1973).

Back in 1958, when Charles Percy was made president of Bell and Howell, he was still under 40. He had come up through the ranks, arriving a few short years before as a trainee. An energetic reporter decided to see if he could find out how Percy had risen so fast. He asked as many people as he could find who had known Percy from the very first days why they thought he had succeeded so quickly. Always the answer was the same: "Because from the very beginning, he showed a knack of being able to get people to make the most of themselves."

In his book about managing a non-profit organization, Peter F. Drucker stresses the importance of developing the people who work with you. He gives this example of a leader who developed people:

One of the most successful developers of people I know is the pastor of a large church. An amazing number of first-rate leaders have come out of his church, so I once asked him to explain how his church he become the breeding ground, the cradle of volunteer leaders. He told me the church tries to provide four things to young people who show up for services: (1) a mentor to guide him or her; (2) a teacher to develop skills; (3) a judge to evaluate progress; and finally, (4) an encourager to cheer them on. (1990, 148)

The pastor told Drucker that the encourager had to be the person at the top, so that is the role that he had assumed. During the years when I served as president of ICI, Global University, and Network211, we had hundreds of people work with us. Many came with great skills already developed, but others came without developed skills. One of our joys was to help them develop attitudes, work habits, and skills that hopefully have stayed with them throughout their lives.

Third, group life demands guidelines. When guidelines are omitted, people will ultimately despise you because they will feel insecure. They will always be wondering whether or not a given action is appropriate and will be accepted. Without the discipline of some guidelines, people are short-changed. Sometimes discipline in the sense of punishment is required.

The writer of Hebrews says, '"For those whom the Lord loves He disciplines, And He scourges every son whom He receives" (Heb. 12:6). We may regard this as a hard saying. We do not want to be disciplined; but once we have been, we can look back on it with joy. When we feel responsible, we have a much healthier outlook on ourselves and life.

Although discipline is needed, every organization also needs the discipline of periodically reducing its guidelines to what is really necessary. The tendency is for the "manual" to grow without discipline. Often, individual cases are used to support unneeded general rules that apply to everyone.

Fourth, people want to be a part of something and to share genuinely in its progress. A sense of belonging and mutual respect develops. Not only do people want us to serve them, they want to serve as well. This illustration about service was in *Bits and Pieces* in July, 1973.

> The great violinist, Nicolo Paganini, willed his marvelous violin to Genoa—the city of his birth—but only on condition that the instrument never be played upon. It was an unfortunate condition, for it is a peculiarity of wood that as long as it is used and handled, it shows little wear. As soon as it is discarded, it begins to decay. The exquisite, mellow-toned violin has become worm-eaten in its beautiful case, valueless except as a relic. The moldering instrument is a reminder that life—withdrawn from all service to others—loses its meaning.

We serve well when we inspire others to serve. When we realize this, we will not be reluctant to call upon others for help in meeting the needs of people around them.

Fifth, vision is an essential ingredient of leadership. A key question is "Where does vision come from?" Henry and Richard Blackaby discuss several sources of vision including the following: (1) copying the leader's own previous success or the success of others, (2) the core values of the organization, and (3) developing vision based on the perceived needs of people to be served (2011, 85-103). While they recognize these human sources, they put the highest priority on the vision originating with God through revelation. They affirm that:

There is a significant difference between revelation and vision. Vision is something people produce. Revelation is something people receive. God must reveal his will if leaders are to know it. The secular world rejects God's will, so nonbelievers are left with one alternative —to project their own vision. Christians are called to a totally different agenda, which is set by God alone. . . . The visions driving spiritual leaders must originate from God. (2011, 103)

Although we all want our vision to originate in the mind of God, we must recognize that we often receive that vision through a divine-human process. As the writer of Proverbs 16:9 says, "The mind of man plans his way, But the Lord directs his steps."

Very often, God gives us a vision that seems too big for us to handle. Indeed, without God, it is, but with God all things are possible. When we are sure that God has spoken, we need not be uneasy about getting it done. Tead maintains that:

The bigger the setting and the meaning in terms of which each leadership situation can be imaginatively conducted, the stronger will be the leader and the more compelling his inspiration.

For where strong faith in the particular effort is present and is imparted, it has its own inner power of infection. It has a compulsion which is transmitted, for it pervades every act of the leader and gives him that which others long to have. (1935, 259)

Unless God is clearly leading, perhaps we should temper Tead's comment with the thought that the vision must not be so large that followers have no hope of implementing it. In other words, we as leaders must work within the range of what is possible. All too often, however, people of small insight wrap the cloak of impossibility around objectives that, with faith, are entirely achievable.

Sixth, we as leaders must be quick to appreciate, applaud, and honor others when they perform well. The observant leader will look for moments to do this in sincerity. If he is not sincere, it will just be manipulation. The manipulator eventually stirs up resentment. We will have ample opportunities, however, to compliment others in all sincerity.

Conclusion

The ministry of Jesus focused on need. We read in Luke 5:30-32: "And the Pharisees and their scribes began grumbling at His disciples, saying, 'Why do you eat and drink with the tax-gatherers and sinners?' And Jesus answered and said to them, 'It is not those who are well who need a physician, but those who are sick. I have not come to call the righteous but sinners to repentance.'"

We must realize, however, that the terms "servant" and "slave" are used by Jesus in the Matthew story in a specialized and paradoxical sense. The important point is that we are meeting the real needs of people, not that we are subject to every whim and want of the people we serve. To do so would be to abdicate the calling to lead that God has given to us.

The challenge to all who would be leaders is to meet needs. By meeting needs, we serve those who would follow us. There is a great cost in meeting needs. This is why Jesus began his response to James and John by focusing on the price of leadership. However, when we see people happily serving the Lord, the price is worth the cost. The harvest is the reward.

CHAPTER TEN

A RANSOM FOR MANY

Introduction

Jesus addressed his remarks in Matthew 20:26-28 to people who would be great and to those who would be first. The world interprets being great and first in terms of position, honor, and power. Jesus inverted this order and interpreted greatness and being first in terms of service. We can be great by serving without power and its related elements.

Leadership and greatness are not synonymous terms, but they are overlapping concepts. We often think, for example, of great leaders. Or, we think people are great because they have extraordinary influence as leaders. Thus, our text becomes a story which raises many leadership issues. All these issues challenge us to think profoundly about what is involved in leading people. The central point of the Matthew story is that service is the indispensable factor in Christian leadership.

In chapter one, we indicated that people could be leaders in the sense of being *"ahead," "a head,"* or *"the head."* One can be *"ahead,"* for example, in service without being *"a head"* or *"the head."* Service is the indispensable factor in all three types of servant leadership. However, our discussions of leadership have focused primarily on the latter two types of leadership—being *"a head"* or *"the head"* of a group. With regard to them, I presented my own definition of leadership.

The desire to be a leader, when service is the indispensable element is a laudable ambition in life. As long as service is put uppermost, the desire to lead is honorable. Service may lead to position and honor, but if not, remember that servanthood is itself a position and that this position has its own greatness in the kingdom of God.

Those who would lead through service do well when they remember that the ultimate in service is to lay down one's life for others. Our text for this book, Matthew 20:20-28, concludes with the example of Jesus as a ransom for many. We will present the entire text and then will focus on verse 28.

> [20]Then the mother of the sons of Zebedee came to Jesus with her sons, bowing down and making a request of Him.

²¹And He said to her, "What do you wish?"

She said to Him, "Command that in Your kingdom these two sons of mine may sit one on Your right and one on Your left."

²²But Jesus answered, "You do not know what you are asking. Are you able to drink the cup that I am about to drink?" They said to Him, "We are able."

²³He said to them, "My cup you shall drink; but to sit on My right and on *My* left, this is not Mine to give, but it is for those for whom it has been prepared by My Father."

²⁴And hearing *this*, the ten became indignant with the two brothers.

²⁵But Jesus called them to Himself and said, "You know that the rulers of the Gentiles lord it over them, and *their* great men exercise authority over them.

²⁶It is not this way among you, but whoever wishes to become great among you shall be your servant.

²⁷and whoever wishes to be first among you shall be your slave;

²⁸just as the Son of Man did not come to be served, but to serve, and to give His life a ransom for many."

Verse 28 brings to mind the various theories of atonement. There is a sense in which the atoning work of Christ includes His service as well as His sacrifice of His life. Indeed, we might say it includes all that He did from His incarnation to the resurrection. However, we normally focus on the atonement as specifically referring to the death of Christ upon the cross.

There are many theories of the atonement. A full description may draw from several theories, but most evangelicals see the atonement as the vicarious sacrifice of Christ for us in satisfying the demands of the justice of God concerning our sins. Christ is a substitute for us; He took our place upon the cross to atone for our sins. I believe this to be the best explanation.

Jesus is our ideal model in service as well as in all other aspects of life. As a ransom for many, He atoned for our sins, doing what no other person could do. However, we can commit our lives fully to Him. We can follow Him in devoted service. Our topics in this chapter will be (1) the service of Christ and ourselves, (2) Christ as the ransom for us, and (3) our actions as followers of Christ.

Concerning Service

Jesus, the Son of Man, "did not come to be served, but to serve." The phrases "to be served" and "to serve" are translations of forms of the Greek verb *diakoneō* (διακονέω). This verb and the noun *diakonos* (διάκονος) refer to serving or service of any kind. Waiters on tables, deacons, and ministers of the Gospel are all included. Several points are relevant.

First, Jesus ministered in many ways to the people around Him. Early in His ministry (Luke 4:18-19), Jesus revealed His ministry agenda in the synagogue at Nazareth. He stood up to read, turned to Isaiah, and read this passage:

> [18]"THE SPIRIT OF THE LORD IS UPON ME, BECAUSE HE ANOINTED ME TO PREACH THE GOSPEL TO THE POOR. HE HAS SENT ME TO PROCLAIM RELEASE TO THE CAPTIVES, AND RECOVERY OF SIGHT TO THE BLIND, TO SET FREE THOSE WHO ARE OPPRESSED, [19]TO PROCLAIM THE FAVORABLE YEAR OF THE LORD."[2]

The agenda of Jesus was to bring deliverance to the people in all aspects of their lives. He had the best interests of the people at heart. He knew what they really needed and sought to serve those interests. He did not pander to their baser instincts nor waste His energy in meeting frivolous needs. True service—true ministry—is devoted to the needs of people which really enhance their lives. Ministry which focuses on such needs will always be strong.

Second, Christ did not come to be ministered to, but His disciples, on their own initiative, did minister to Him. We, too, can minister to the Lord. Let's observe some of the Biblical evidence.

One. The Old Testament speaks of ministry to God. Concerning the Levites, we read in 1 Chronicles 15:2: "Then David said, 'No one is to carry the ark of God but the Levites; for the Lord chose them to carry the ark of God, and to minister to Him forever.'" Similarly, in 1 Chronicles 23:13 we read about Aaron and his sons: "The sons of Amram were Aaron and Moses. And Aaron was set apart to sanctify him as most holy, he and his sons forever, to burn incense before the Lord, to minister to Him and to bless in His name forever." Aaron and

---

[2] NOTE: In the NASB95 translation, quotations from the Old Testament are presented in uppercase letters.

his sons ministered to the Lord through the burning of incense. The Psalmist emphasizes praise. In Psalm 56:12 (KJV), he writes, "I will render praises unto thee."

Two. Although our text emphasizes Christ's ministry to others, we do have some evidence in the New Testament that He accepted ministry to Himself. A couple of examples will illustrate how the disciples ministered to Him. As one example, a company of women travelled with Jesus and the twelve disciples. These women ministered to Jesus through their gifts. We read about this in Luke 8:1-3:

> [1]Soon afterwards, He *began* going around from one city and village to another, proclaiming and preaching the kingdom of God. The twelve were with Him,
> [2]and *also* some women who had been healed of evil spirits and sicknesses: Mary who was called Magdalene, from whom seven demons had gone out,
> [3]and Joanna the wife of Chuza, Herod's steward, and Susanna, and many others who were contributing to their support out of their private means.

The word "contributing" is a translation of a form of *diakoneō* which, as noted above, means to minister or to serve. They ministered to Jesus and the twelve by giving of their possessions to help the cause.

Another example is that one evening during supper Jesus accepted the ministry of Mary. As John 12:3 records: "Mary therefore took a pound of very costly perfume of pure nard, and anointed the feet of Jesus and wiped His feet with her hair; and the house was filled with the fragrance of the perfume."

Judas Iscariot, the treasurer, objected to Mary's action, saying that the perfume should have been sold and the money given to the poor. Really, he was not concerned about the poor. He was the keeper of the money box, and it was his practice to pilfer from it. Jesus approved Mary's action and said, "For you always have the poor with you, but you do not always have Me" (John 12:8).

Another way the disciples ministered to Christ is through helping others. When we help others, we minister to the Lord

Himself. Jesus taught His disciples this truth in Matthew 25:31-46 where we read these comments:

[31]But when the Son of Man comes in His glory, and all the angels with Him, then He will sit on His glorious throne.

[32]All the nations will be gathered before Him; and He will separate them from one another, as the shepherd separates the sheep from the goats;

[33]and He will put the sheep on His right, and the goats on the left.

[34]Then the King will say to those on His right, "Come, you who are blessed of My Father, inherit the kingdom prepared for you from the foundation of the world.

[35]For I was hungry, and you gave Me *something* to eat; I was thirsty, and you gave Me *something* to drink; I was a stranger, and you invited Me in;

[36]naked, and you clothed Me; I was sick, and you visited Me; I was in prison, and you came to Me."

[37]Then the righteous will answer Him, "Lord, when did we see You hungry, and feed You, or thirsty, and give You *something* to drink?

[38]And when did we see You a stranger, and invite You in, or naked, and clothe You?

[39]When did we see You sick, or in prison, and come to You?"

[40]The King will answer and say to them, "Truly I say to you, to the extent that you did it to one of these brothers of Mine, *even* the least *of them*, you did it to Me."

[41]Then He will also say to those on His left, 'Depart from Me, accursed ones, into the eternal fire which has been prepared for the devil and his angels;

[42]for I was hungry, and you gave Me *nothing* to eat; I was thirsty, and you gave Me nothing to drink;

[43]I was a stranger, and you did not invite Me in; naked, and you did not clothe Me; sick, and in prison, and you did not visit Me."

[44]Then they themselves also will answer, "Lord, when did we see You hungry, or thirsty, or a stranger, or naked, or sick, or in prison, and did not take care of You?"

[45]Then He will answer them, 'Truly I say to you, to the extent that you did not do it to one of the least of these, you did not do it to Me."

[46]These will go away into eternal punishment, but the righteous into eternal life.

Christ came to minister to others. Thus, our ministry to others harmonizes directly with the purpose for which Christ came. He is our model. It is important for us to see Christ in the faces of the people to whom we minister. Sometimes we help others when we are not sure they are deserving of help. Even so, we must do it as unto Christ. Our help could be a step toward their redemption.

Christ as Ransom

Our text says that Jesus came "to give His life a ransom for many." The apostle Paul adds that "God was in Christ reconciling the world to Himself" (2 Cor. 5:19). Both the Father and the Son are involved in the redemption of man. They acted out of their own will and compassion.

First, the word "ransom" is a translation of the Greek word *lutron* (λύτρον). This Greek word is used in the New Testament only here, in the parallel passage in Mark 10:45, and in 1 Timothy 2:6. Before discussing Christ as a ransom, we will consider the general meaning of the term *lutron.*

According to W. E. Vine, a *lutron* (ransom) is a means of loosing. Because of this, *lutron* "is used of the 'ransom' for a life, e.g. Ex. 21:30, of the redemption price of a slave, e.g. Lev. 19:20, of land, 25:24, of the price of a captive, Isa. 45:13" (1996, 506). Similarly, Morris, in the *New Bible Dictionary* says the purpose of a ransom is to bring about redemption. Through redemption, a person is delivered from some evil. Three examples are given: (1) prisoners of war might be released on payment of a price which was called a "ransom;" (2) slaves might be released by a process of ransom in which they paid their masters for freedom; and (3) among the Hebrews, one who commits an unpremeditated murder (Exod. 21:28-30) might redeem his forfeited life with a price. (1982, 1013).

Second, Jesus described Himself as a "ransom for many." It is important to consider both the application of the term "ransom" to Christ and the term "many." These two terms give us the hope of eternal life because Christ brought about our deliverance from sin and our separation unto God.

One. Applying the concept of ransom to Christ, Vine writes: "That Christ gave up His life in expiatory sacrifice under God's judgment upon sin and thus provided a 'ransom' whereby those who receive Him on this ground obtain deliverance from the penalty due to sin, is what Scripture teaches" (1996, 506). The term *expiation* means "to cover" or "to cleanse" sin. Through Christ's sacrifice, our sins are cancelled.

Morris writes, "He [God] makes known His strength. Because He loves His people He redeems them at cost to Himself. His effort is regarded as the 'price'" (1982, 1013). Going further, the author states: "When we read of 'redemption through his blood' (Eph. 1:7), the blood of Christ is clearly being regarded as the price of redemption" (1982, 1014).

Two. Jesus said He was a ransom for "many." Some interpreters believe that Christ died only for those who accept Him. However, by using the term "many," Jesus does not exclude anyone. Elsewhere Paul makes it clear that Jesus died for all. In 1 Timothy 2:5-6, Paul writes: "For there is one God, *and* one mediator also between God and men, *the* man Christ Jesus, who gave Himself as a ransom for all, the testimony given at the proper time." Jesus died for all people and paid the ransom for them, but all people do not accept Him. Although the price is paid, many people tragically reject Christ and do not avail themselves of the free gift of salvation.

Third, throughout church history, the question has been asked, "To whom was the price of Christ's life paid?" The theories of atonement include several answers to this question.

One. As Leon Morris points out, the early church Fathers tended to answer that the price was paid to "Satan." Morris writes:

Some of them worked out quite a theory of the way redemption works. They held that because of our sin we were all destined for hell. Sinners belong to Satan. In that situation God, in effect, offered to do a deal with Satan. He would give his Son in exchange for sinners. Satan realized that he would be making a fine profit on this transaction and was happy to accept the offer. The death of Jesus on the cross represented the handing of the Son over to Satan. But when Satan got Jesus down into hell he found (in the modern elegant idiom) that he had bitten off more than he could chew. On the third day Christ rose triumphant and Satan was left lamenting, having lost both the sinners he previously had and him whom he had accepted in exchange for them. (1983, 129)

This view has little support, if any, today. God was not obligated to Satan for anything. Moreover, God is all-powerful and had no need of paying a ransom to someone else to achieve His objective.

Two. According to Morris, the word *ransom* means that Christ gave His life as a price, but the New Testament does not name a recipient of the price. He declares that:

> In the New Testament there is never any hint of a recipient of the ransom. In other words we must understand redemption as a useful metaphor which enables us to see some aspects of Christ's great saving work with clarity but which is not an exact description of the whole process of salvation. We must not press it beyond what the New Testament tells us about it. To look for a recipient of the ransom is illegitimate. We have no reason for pressing every detail. We must use the metaphor in the way the New Testament writers did or we fall into error.
>
> This does not mean that we should water down the meaning of redemption. It is necessary for us to see the main thrust of the metaphor. This way of looking at the cross brings out the magnitude of the price paid for our salvation. It shows us that the death of Christ was meaningful. It was more than the martyrdom of a good man who was not strong enough to resist the machinations of evil people. Rather it was the outworking of the love of God. It was God's costly way of overcoming evil. Looked at in this way Christ's death was the effective payment that removed our bondage to evil. (1983, 129-130)

Three. Other interpreters, such as R. W. Lyon, seem to go further. Lyon rejects the idea of the ransom of Christ being a transaction with a price. Rather, he puts the emphasis on the power of the cross to deliver men from their bondage and sins. He states:

> The ideas [about ransom] are rooted in the ancient world where slaves and captured soldiers were given their freedom upon the payment of a price. In the OT ransom is linked again with slaves, but also with varied aspects of the cultures as well as the duties of kinsmen (cf. Ruth 4). Most importantly the idea of ransom (redeem) is also linked with the deliverance out of Egypt (e.g.,

Deut. 7:8) and the return of the exiles (e.g. Isa. 35:10). In both settings the focus is no longer on the price paid but on the deliverance achieved and the freedom obtained. Now the focus is on the activity of God and his power to set his people free. When the ideas of ransom are linked to the saving activity of God, the idea of price is not present.

When the NT, therefore, speaks of ransom with reference to the work of Christ, the idea is not one of transaction, as though a deal is arranged and a price paid. Rather the focus is on the power (I Cor. 1:18) of the cross to save. In the famous ransom saying of Mark 10:45 Jesus speaks of his coming death as the means of release for many. The contrast is between his own solitary death and the deliverance of the many. In the NT the terms of ransom and purchase, which in other contexts suggest an economic or financial exchange, speak of the consequences or results (cf. I Cor. 7:23). The release is from judgment (Rom. 3:25-26), sin (Eph. 1:7), death (Rom. 8:2). (1984, 907-908)

Four. Another view, which I accept, is that the price was paid to God. Hebrews 9:14 gives some support to this approach. Here, we read: "For if the blood of goats and bulls and the ashes of a heifer sprinkling those who have been defiled sanctify for the cleansing of the flesh, how much more will the blood of Christ, who through the eternal Spirit offered Himself without blemish to God, cleanse your conscience from dead works to serve the living God?" We note that Christ offered Himself "to God." He did this in order to atone for our sins.

Other passages indicate that Jesus "bought" us. Acts 20:28 speaks about the "church of God which He purchased with His own blood." In addition, Paul says in 1 Corinthians 6:20 that "you have been bought with a price" (compare 1 Cor. 7:23). Although these passages do not specifically say that the price was paid to God, they certainly harmonize with this position.

Because the ransom is an aspect of the atonement, an issue arises concerning the ransom and the penal substitution view of the atonement. The question is: "Does the penal substitution view require that the price was paid to God?" As stated above, Morris holds that a price was paid for our redemption, but that a recipient is not named. However, the view that the ransom was paid to God certainly harmonizes with the penal substitution view.

The vicarious substitution position is that God is just and, because He is just, the penalty for sin had to be paid. This price was necessary in order for God to sustain the moral order of His universe. Consequently, Christ died as a substitute for us. Because men have sinned, they should pay the penalty, but God chose to pay it Himself in order to redeem them.

Some people believe that substitutionary atonement is immoral and unjust. It would be unjust, they say, for an innocent party to be sentenced by a court and be punished for a guilty person. However, as Millard Erickson states:

> There are two answers to this objection. One is the voluntary character of the sacrifice. . . . Jesus was not compelled by the Father to lay down his life. He did so voluntarily and thus pleased the Father. It hardly need be said that taking someone who willingly volunteers is preferable to conscripting someone for punishment.
>
> The second answer is that the work of Jesus Christ in giving his life also involved the Father. . . . In terms of our courtroom analogy, it is not as if the judge passes sentence on the defendant, and some innocent and hitherto uninvolved party then appears to pay the fine or serve the sentence. Rather, it is as if the judge passes sentence upon the defendant, then removes his robes and goes off to serve the sentence in the defendant's place. (1983, 817)

Followers of Christ

As followers of Christ, how shall we act? Our answer involves our own needs, the gifts God has given us to minster to others, our role with regard to Christ as the ransom, and the redemptive purpose of leadership.

First, because we are completely human, we have great needs. Jesus came to meet those needs. As leaders, we must recognize that we have needs and be willing to accept help when we need it. We must receive ministry as well as give ministry. Sometimes our pride keeps us from receiving what we need. We must remember that even Christ accepted the ministrations of His disciples.

Second, as Christian leaders, our purpose is to minister to others. Just as Christ came to minister, we must put our emphasis on ministry.

We should not make position and honor our highest priority. Whatever role God has for us, we should accept it and serve well.

God has given us a whole constellation of gifts with which to minister. We read about them in Romans 12:1-8, Ephesians 4:11-12, and 1 Corinthians 12:1-31. The Spirit of God distributes the gifts as He desires, but no one is left out (1 Cor. 12:11). If anyone should think he has been overlooked, he should read 1 Corinthians 12:28 where "helps" is named. Everyone can exercise this gift! Some people, however, are especially outstanding in being a help to others in virtually every situation.

Third, at this point, we might ask, "In what sense can we follow Christ in being a 'ransom' for many?" Obviously, we cannot atone for sins. Only Christ was worthy to pay the price to satisfy the justice of God. In addition, the writer of Hebrews tells us that Christ was "offered once to bear the sins of many" (9:28). The price is paid for all, and it is paid for all eternity. Christ will not have to pay the price again.

We are not required to do what Christ alone could do. We can, however, pay the price of fulfilling our role in the kingdom of God. All of us, for example, are to be witnesses to the redeeming work of Christ. The ministry of witnessing can exact a great price. For example, there is the price of being looked down upon by segments of our society. In many countries, the price is much greater.

Throughout the history of the church, many witnesses have given their lives for the cause of Christ. The English word witness is translated from the Greek word *martus* (μάρτυς). This word is sometimes translated as "martyr." The connection is not accidental. Many of the early witnesses became martyrs. Today, across the world, there are many witnesses who become martyrs.

Fourth, we have been saying that the indispensable element of Christian leadership is service. People may serve for many reasons, but we must add that the purpose of service in Christian leadership is redemption. Richard Wolff lays the foundation for this thought with these comments: "The ultimate purpose of Christ was redemptive. . . . Through redemption, man is set free from the controlling power of sin, thus enabled to *serve* God and man" (1970, 34). Then, he says: "True Christian leadership is redemptive, i.e. liberating! The purpose is never to enslave or to subjugate" (1970, 35).

Conclusion

God could have chosen to disdain man, to create other creatures who would serve Him, or to abide alone in all His glory. Instead, He chose to take on the form of man and to dwell among us in the person of Christ (John 1:14; Phil. 2:5-11). He did this in order that He might lead us out of bondage into freedom. Because Christ was willing to suffer and to die, He will reign as King of Kings and Lord of Lords!

Several points stand out. One, Christ, the Second Person of the Godhead, was ultimately worthy to be the sacrifice for sins. He was without sin! Two, Christ paid the ultimate sacrifice. He emptied Himself and became man. He took upon Himself the form of a slave or bond-servant (*doulou*, slave). Then, He suffered and died for us. Three, Christ is the ultimate leader. He rose from the grave and is the head of the church. He is coming back in power and in glory to be the King.

Christ was unique! We cannot match Him in any way, but we can follow His example. Paul exhorts us to: "Have this attitude in yourselves which was also in Christ Jesus" (Phil. 2:5). When we have the attitude of Christ, we will be willing to pay any price to tell the story of redemption.

Paul's Example. The apostle Paul is an example for us. He said, "I bear on my body the brand-marks [*stigmata*] of Jesus" (Gal. 6:17). Paul bore the literal scars on his body of his many beatings. In addition, he bore the marks in a figurative way. The word "brand-marks" is a translation of the Greek word *stigmata* (στίγματα). We take our English word *stigma* from this Greek word. Paul accepted the stigma of the cross and was a faithful witness.

Our Lord calls upon us to invest our lives in redemptive service. Through our service, people are blessed and their lives are changed. Sometimes this service demands a price, but we can be confident that our Lord will reward us. We have a great future! The apostle Paul, who was both a leader and was great, declared: "If we endure, we shall also reign with Him" (2 Tim. 2:12).

CHAPTER ELEVEN

THE CALL OF GOD TO SERVE

Introduction

Another leadership issue that arises in connection with Matthew's story is "the call of God to serve." God takes the initiative and calls believers to serve in specific roles and to perform given tasks. In the New Testament, this call is an aspect of the calling of God in general. The terms "call" and "calling" mainly have a much broader meaning. In a general sense, these terms refer to salvation and all its aspects. Through God's call, He communicates to you the message of what He wants you to be and to do.

When God calls us in the broader sense, He summons us to all aspects of our lives as followers of Christ. Paul says that we are "the called of Jesus Christ" (Rom. 1:6). Most of the Scriptures dealing with our calling are general in nature (e.g. Rom. 11:29; Phil. 3:14; Eph. 4:1). However, some of the Scriptures highlight a specific characteristic of our calling. Paul writes, for example, about God "who has saved us and called us with a holy calling" (2 Tim. 1:9). Similarly, he declares that believers "have been sanctified in Christ Jesus" and that they are "saints by calling" (1 Cor. 1:2). In these verses, Paul stresses the holiness of our calling.

When we speak about the call of God to serve, we have in mind a narrower use of the term "call of God." All believers, in a sense, are called to serve, but each believer may serve in a different way. Thus, a commonly used meaning of this term is that a person is not only called to serve, but also to a special calling. Very often, this is a call to lead by serving. God not only invites us to a given role, but He also urges us to do it. Because God wants us to do something, we can have confidence that He will enable us to do it.

Used in this way, "the call of God" frequently has the connotation of an individual being called to a task. One who is called of God to a prophetic role will likely be quite individualistic. However, individuals can be called to function in relationship to groups as well. When called to do something with or in a group, ways to work together must become a part of the outworking of the call. Also, groups can be called of God to given tasks.

The term "called of God" is widely used by believers in connection with service. With regard to our service, we consider it important to be called. Recently, we attended an Assemblies of God World Missions commissioning service for newly appointed or reappointed missionaries. The World Missions Board presented 89 persons for service in 39 countries.

At the appropriate time, Dr. Greg Mundis, the Executive Director, issued this declaration: "Assemblies of God World Missions, duly constituted by the General Council for the commissioning of missionary personnel, has, within the limits of our ability, determined that these people are called of God and qualified for assignment as world missions envoys." The church, including Pentecostals, has long stressed the importance of the call of God. That emphasis includes, though it is not limited to, a special call to vocational ministry. Very often, the call is to full-time ministry, but people who are not full time are called as well.

Jesus issues a call to service in the Matthew story. The story begins with the desires of James and John, supported by their mother, to be great and to have positions of honor. Jesus does not rebuke them, but He shows them how to become great through service. In effect, Jesus issues a call to service. The call to service becomes the call of God for their lives. As in each previous chapter, I will cite the entire story in Matthew 20:20-28. Verses 21, 23, 26, and 27 are especially relevant with regard to the call of God to serve.

> [20]Then the mother of the sons of Zebedee came to Jesus with her sons, bowing down and making a request of Him.
>
> [21]And He said to her, "What do you wish?"
> She said to Him, "Command that in Your kingdom these two sons of mine may sit one on Your right and one on Your left."
>
> [22]But Jesus answered, "You do not know what you are asking. Are you able to drink the cup that I am about to drink?" They said to Him, "We are able."
>
> [23]He said to them, "My cup you shall drink; but to sit on My right and on *My* left, this is not Mine to give, but it is for those for whom it has been prepared by My Father."
>
> [24]And hearing *this*, the ten became indignant with the two brothers.

²⁵But Jesus called them to Himself and said, "You know that the rulers of the Gentiles lord it over them, and *their* great men exercise authority over them.

²⁶It is not this way among you, but whoever wishes to become great among you shall be your servant.

²⁷and whoever wishes to be first among you shall be your slave;

²⁸just as the Son of Man did not come to be served, but to serve, and to give His life a ransom for many."

The Desire and the Call

There are several verses in the Matthew story that raise the issue of the desire to lead and the call to serve. The mother of James and John asked for positions of honor (verse 21). Then Jesus told them and the other disciples that these positions were set aside for those for whom they had been prepared. Later in the story, Jesus addressed those who would be great and said to them that they must be a servant (verse 26). Moreover, the one who would be first must be a slave. Concerning the desire to lead and the call of God, we note the following thoughts.

First, the disciples, including James and John, were not strangers to the call of God. Jesus was walking by the Sea of Galilee when He saw Simon and Andrew his brother casting a net into the Sea because they were fishermen. Jesus made His presence known to them. Matthew says (4:18-22):

¹⁸Now as Jesus was walking by the Sea of Galilee, He saw two brothers, Simon who was called Peter, and Andrew his brother, casting a net into the sea; for they were fishermen.

¹⁹And He said to them, "Follow Me and I will make you fishers of men."

²⁰Immediately they left their nets and followed Him.

²¹Going on from there He saw two other brothers, James the *son* of Zebedee, and John his brother, in the boat with Zebedee their father, mending their nets; and He called them.

²²Immediately they left their boat and their father, and followed Him. (Compare Mark 1:19-20 and Luke 5:10)

Obviously, James and John, along with Peter and Andrew, were "fishers of men." The disciples began with service, especially with drawing people to Christ and His cause. Somewhere along the line during their service, they began to think in terms of honor and position.

When Jesus and the disciples were on the way to Jerusalem, they made the request to sit on the right and left hands of Jesus.

Second, on the one hand, Jesus said: "My cup you shall drink; but to sit on My right and on *My* left, this is not Mine to give, but it is for those for whom it has been prepared by My Father" (20:23). The last clause raises the issue of destiny in connection with the call of God.

When God destines a person for a given service role, He takes a strong and sovereign action. Moreover, that destiny becomes the person's calling. The destined person responds positively to God's call. One can be destined for service without knowing it, but over time that destiny will become known, especially through the service. Very often, while serving, a person comes to the realization that he or she is destined for service.

The term "call of God" often has to do with God communicating His will to us. Although a person can have a calling without knowing it, we assume that normally God will make his calling known. Eventually He does. When He speaks to us, we have a conviction that He is working His will. Normally this is accompanied by a strong desire to fulfill that role. A person fully submitted to God wants to do what God wills.

Third, on the other hand, Jesus said, "whoever wishes to become great among you shall be your servant" (20:26) and "whoever wishes to be first among you shall be your slave" (20:27). In contrast to the destiny mentioned in verse 23, these verses talk about the desire of the disciples to be great and to lead. The emphasis here is on the free will of the disciples. Jesus issued a challenge to them—if they would be great, they must be servants. Going further, if they would be first, they must be slaves.

The challenge that Jesus presented constitutes, in a sense, the call of God. God calls the disciples to serve, and they answer the call. Normally, there will be the added step of hearing the call of God to a given role. So the steps to the call of God are the desire to lead, Jesus' challenge to serve, and finding God's will for a more specific role. God, taking the initiative, issues the call. We answer the call and God empowers us for the task.

When a believer is trying to determine his or her service role, the human side is the desire to lead and the divine side is the call of God. The desire to lead and the call of God sometimes go together, but not always. Either the desire to lead or the call of God can precede the other. When a person is called of God to lead, he usually will want to lead. When a person wants to lead, God may call him to lead, but not always.

The Need and the Call

A discussion of the call of God to serve presupposes that there is a need to be met. In other words, there is a purpose and reason for our service. Meeting the need is how we will serve. Consequently, the call of God often focuses on a specific need or needs that He wants us to meet. He also gives us a spiritual burden to meet the need and shows us how. God helps us to see the need and then calls us to help meet the need. When God shows us the need, imparts a spiritual burden to meet the need, and gives us the solution—this constitutes the call of God to serve.

In the fall of 1998, Esther and I were attending the missions convention at Christian Life Assembly in Carrollton, Texas. We were developing plans for a global evangelism and discipleship outreach via the Internet. We saw the need to use the Internet as a tool of evangelism. Originally, we called the outreach Global Colleagues, but it later became known as Network211. The numerals 211 mean that we are using 21st century technology to communicate the 1st century gospel.

During the Sunday morning service, we happened to be on the front row and were standing for worship with the rest of the congregation. Although I was not really involved in the worship, I began to tremble, and tears welled up in my eyes. Then I felt that I heard the voice of the Spirit speaking the words "ten million" to my mind and heart. I interpreted that to mean that the Lord would help us reach ten million people with the gospel. Later we set a goal of reaching ten million people in ten years. With the help of the Lord, we reached that goal in five years.

As we developed the outreach, we launched a web site that focuses on felt needs that people have worldwide. These are needs that people have on their journey through life. So we called the web site *journeyanswers.com*. We now have this web site in the world's top ten Internet languages as well as others. We have other web sites also. As of this writing, our goal is to reach one hundred million people. We look forward to the day when that goal is greatly revised upward.

God Calling

The Matthew story is about James and John who wanted positions of honor. Jesus used their desires to teach them that greatness comes through service and issued them a call to serve. However, the Bible has many examples of God calling people to given tasks whether they initially wanted to get involved or not. Thus, at this point, it will be helpful to look at some Biblical examples of people who were called of God to serve in specific roles. From these examples, we will learn that God sometimes calls in dramatic ways. As we observe these callings, we note that the Scriptures often describe a "call" without using the term "call of God."

First, Abram, who became Abraham, was called by God to be the one through whom all the families of the earth would be blessed. God initially called Abraham when he was living in Mesopotamia. Speaking to the high priest, Stephen, in Acts 7:2-4, said:

> ²And he said, "Hear me, brethren and fathers! The God of glory appeared to our father Abraham when he was in Mesopotamia, before he lived in Haran,
> ³and said to him, 'LEAVE YOUR COUNTRY AND YOUR RELATIVES, AND COME INTO THE LAND THAT I WILL SHOW YOU.'³
> ⁴Then he left the land of the Chaldeans and settled in Haran. From there, after his father died, *God* had him move to this country in which you are now living.

After Abraham's father died, when Abraham was living in Haran, God spoke to Abraham again. This time the record does not tell us that God appeared to Abraham. However, according to Genesis 12:1-3, God spoke to Abraham. The event is reported as follows:

> ¹Now the LORD said to Abram, "Go forth from your country, And from your relatives And from your father's house, To the land which I will show you;
> ²And I will make you a great nation, And I will bless you, And make your name great; And so you shall be a blessing;
> ³And I will bless those who bless you, And the one who curses you I will curse. And in you all the families of the earth will be blessed."

Second, God called Moses to lead the children of Israel out of Egypt and to rule over them during the years they were in the wilderness. Moses took the flock of Jethro, his father-in-law, to the west side of the wilderness and came to mount Horeb when something dramatic

---

³NOTE: In the NASB95 translation, quotations from the Old Testament are presented in uppercase letters.

happened. According to Exodus 3:2, "The angel of the LORD appeared to him in a blazing fire from the midst of a bush; and he looked, and behold, the bush was burning with fire, yet the bush was not consumed." Moses "turned aside" to look at what happened. At this point, as reported in Exodus 3:4, 5, and 10, God called Moses to his task of delivering Israel. These verses say:

4 When the LORD saw that he turned aside to look, God called to him from the midst of the bush and said, "Moses, Moses!" And he said, "Here I am."

5 Then He said, "Do not come near here; remove your sandals from your feet, for the place on which you are standing is holy ground."

----

10 "Therefore, come now, and I will send you to Pharaoh, so that you may bring My people, the sons of Israel, out of Egypt."

Third, when God called Isaiah, he saw a vision with seraphim standing above the Lord. Upon seeing the vision and hearing the seraphim speak, Isaiah declared that he was "a man of unclean lips" (Isa. 6:5). Then one of the seraphim touched his mouth with a burning coal taken from the altar with tongs and announced that Isaiah's iniquity "is taken away and your sin is forgiven" (Isa. 6:7). "Then," as Isaiah 6:8 reports, "I heard the voice of the Lord, saying, 'Whom shall I send, and who will go for Us?' Then I said, 'Here am I. Send me!'"

Fourth, turning now to the New Testament, we read about the sending of the twelve apostles out to minister. Jesus had previously called them to follow Him, but this was a special moment of appointment for ministry. Luke tells us, "1And He called the twelve together, and gave them power and authority over all the demons and to heal diseases. 2And He sent them out to proclaim the kingdom of God and to perform healing" (Luke 9:1-2). Luke does not tell us whether or not anything happened right away that would give evidence of empowerment, but we know that it did when they went out to minister. When they returned, they gave an account to Jesus of their ministry (Luke 9:10).

Fifth, when God wanted to use Peter to take the gospel to the Gentiles at the house of Cornelius, He spoke to Peter through a vision. Three times, God instructed Peter to eat food that He had cleansed.

While Peter was perplexed by what he saw, the men from the house of Cornelius arrived. Then, according to Acts 10:19-20:

> ^{19}While Peter was reflecting on the vision, the Spirit said to him, "Behold, three men are looking for you.
> ^{20}But get up, go downstairs and accompany them without misgivings, for I have sent them Myself."

The essential point is that Peter was to go to the house of Cornelius "without misgivings." It is always a great moment when we know with assurance that God has called us to a given task and that we can perform it with full assurance of God's blessing. This assurance can come through a variety of ways as well as through a dream or a vision.

Sixth, Paul believed and taught that he was called to be an apostle. He was "an apostle of Jesus Christ by the will of God" (1 Cor. 1:1; compare Rom. 1:1 and 1 Cor. 15:9-10). When Paul encountered Christ on the road to Damascus, he was smitten with blindness. However, God spoke to Ananias in a vision saying that Paul saw him in a vision and to go and lay hands on him so that he might receive his sight. Ananias was reluctant to go, but went when God explained what was happening. We read about it in Acts 9:15-19:

> ^{15}But the Lord said to him, "Go, for he is a chosen instrument of Mine, to bear My name before the Gentiles and kings and the sons of Israel;
> ^{16} for I will show him how much he must suffer for My name's sake."
> ^{17}So Ananias departed and entered the house, and after laying his hands on him said, "Brother Saul, the Lord Jesus, who appeared to you on the road by which you were coming, has sent me so that you may regain your sight and be filled with the Holy Spirit."
> ^{18}And immediately there fell from his eyes something like scales, and he regained his sight, and he got up and was baptized;
> ^{19} and he took food and was strengthened.

The callings that I have cited have supernatural elements. I am not suggesting that every call of God in the Bible is like these. Indeed, these examples stand out because of their uniqueness. Many people, no doubt, were called to serve without having such supernatural crisis experiences. Nevertheless, it helps us to know that it is the same God calling us, no matter how He does it. Sometimes He still speaks in dramatic ways, but sometimes in more ordinary modes. God speaks in different ways, but we have the assurance that He does speak. We must follow Him fully, no matter how He speaks.

Hearing God's Call

Many times, we pray that we will hear the call of God and that we will be in the will of God. In 1 Corinthians 1:1, Paul states: "Paul, called as an apostle of Jesus Christ by the will of God." He made it known that it was by the will of God that he was an apostle. The call of God is something He does, whereas the will of God is what He wants. When He calls, He calls according to His will.

When we talk about the call of God, we usually have in mind an event that has lasting impact, but the call is not limited to one event. We have an ongoing relationship with God with many special moments. When we speak about finding the will of God, we often think of an ongoing condition, but we can refer also to a given event or time. God continues to align us with His will and call us to service.

We live with the conviction that God calls us. Moreover, God makes His call known to us in a variety of ways. These ways also are ways that He communicates His will to us. He may reveal His call and will in a special moment or step-by-step over time. Sometimes God calls in surprising ways. Without attempting to write a complete list, I have commented here on some of the ways that God speaks to us.

First, sometimes, when God calls us, our spiritual senses are dramatically engaged; but at other times, we simply commit our lives to God and trust Him to lead. My favorite verse of Scripture is Proverbs 16:9 which says: "The mind of man plans his way, but the Lord directs his steps." God has given us our minds, and we should diligently use them. As we plan for the future, we should do our "homework." While doing this, we must fully submit ourselves to God. We must make a "faith-commitment" to Him. We can do this with confidence that He will lead us. He will make His call known to us as we serve Him.

Second, a few people testify to hearing the audible voice of God, but many more testimonies have to do with the inner voice of the Spirit. The inner voice can be the voice of the Spirit, our own spirit, or our spirit inspired by the Spirit. So that we can be in the center of God's will, our great desire is to hear the inner voice of the Spirit. Fortunately, we can hear the Spirit's voice with our spiritual ears. A. W. Tozer declared, "The soul has eyes with which to see and ears with which to hear. Feeble though they may be from long disuse, but by the life-giving touch of Christ alive now and capable of sharpest sight and most sensitive hearing" (1948, 58). When our spiritual senses are alive, we can know with assurance that God has called.

Third, God may call us by inspiring us with His Word. We must base our lives on the Word of God. The principles and commands of the Bible provide us with the overall guidance that we need to live Christ-centered lives. Obviously, we want to also have specific guidance for our lives. We want to know that we are being and doing what God wants. We are eager for God to communicate with us.

Many times, God quickens our minds when we read His Word. The quickening of the Spirit as we read God's Word can constitute a call. A verse of Scripture often takes on new meaning, and we believe that the verse applies to us. Sometimes, our spiritual eyes see a great truth and the Word of God burns it in our hearts, inspiring us to act. God uses the Word to guide our lives. As the psalmist declares, "Your word is a lamp to my feet And a light to my path" (Ps. 119:105).

Fourth, God may call us by what He does as we pray. As we pray, the Spirit sometimes leads us to examine our own lives. Just as Isaiah was cleansed before God called him, so He can tune up our lives. After cleansing Isaiah, God was able to communicate with Him concerning a call to serve. Similarly, we can be led into the service that God desires for us.

Sometimes we face problems in our ministries. Many times, while we are praying, God will inspire us with the solution. Early in the history of International Correspondence Institute (now Global University), we faced tension over the role of ICI and the Bible schools around the world. Some of the Bible school people felt we would diminish their work. The tension was serious, so I took some time in a room on the Central Bible College campus in Springfield, Missouri, to pray. While on my knees praying, I wrote out our proposed way of working with Bible schools. We created a way for the schools to use our materials for credit with us or without credit. They were able to see us as a blessing rather than diminishing their work. The materials we developed enhanced their work. This became the way we have worked with the schools ever since. This is the way we answered God's call to help the Bible schools.

Many times, we pray to God, listen for His answer, and hear the inner voice of the Spirit speak to us. However, sometimes we feel that He has not spoken as clearly as we would like. Sometimes, we do not know just how to pray, but the Spirit prays through us according to the will of God. Paul writes:

> ²⁶In the same way the Spirit also helps our weakness; for we do not know how to pray as we should, but the Spirit Himself intercedes for *us* with groanings too deep for words;
>
> ²⁷and He who searches the hearts knows what the mind of the Spirit is, because He intercedes for the saints according to *the will of* God (Rom. 8:26-27).

The Spirit may pray about any aspect of our lives. This would include knowing God's will for our service and hearing the call of God. When the Spirit prays through us, we can be confident that He will lead us. Many times, we will hear God speaking with the inner voice of the Spirit.

Fifth, God may call us through the advice of wise counselors. Sometimes, God raises up a prophet, such as Moses, and calls him to act without much consultation with others. However, most of the time, having wise counselors is a helping step in knowing God's will. According to Proverbs 15:22, "Without consultation, plans are frustrated, But with many counselors they succeed." The consultation can help define the shape of the call of God for us.

As I indicated earlier, I proposed the formation of ICI to the leadership of the Foreign Mission Department (now Assemblies of God World Missions) of the General Council of the Assemblies of God. Obviously, we had a lot of meetings with the leaders of the Foreign Missions Department, as well as others. Then, in 1969, my family and I took ten months to make a trip around the world. We visited with many missionary field fellowships. The purpose was to consult with the people on the field and learn what could be workable patterns for the operation of ICI. Through consultation, the nature of our calling was refined. What we learned was invaluable for the entire future life of the school.

Sixth, God may call us through the circumstances of life. All of us are confronted daily with the circumstances of life. We often face decisions that seem to be influenced by factors that we cannot control. Under such circumstances, we sometimes have to yield to the situation and live within the limits of the situation that confronts us. Fortunately, God is in control of all the circumstances. So, sometimes He works in ways well beyond what we can do. When he does, we are blessed by

His miraculous work. He gives us new circumstances to guide our lives. God calls us in a new way.

Seventh, another way that God calls us is by giving spiritual gifts to us. Paul writes: "But to each one is given the manifestation of the Spirit for the common good" (1 Cor. 12:7). Each person has at least one gift. The very giving of the gift becomes a call for us to properly use it. Sometimes, we have to exercise a gift for a while before we realize that God has called us to be used in this way. When it becomes obvious what gift the Spirit has distributed to us, it becomes easy for us to answer His call.

Conclusion

Every believer is called to follow Christ and to experience His life in many dimensions. Used in this way, the term "calling" or "call" of God is broad and quite inclusive of all that we are in Christ. One of the dimensions of our calling is the call to serve. In a sense, all believers are called to serve the Lord. In addition, each believer can serve the Lord in a specific way. The call of God is one of the great evidences of the presence of the Spirit in the life of the church.

James and John wanted positions of honor and power. Rather than rebuking them, Jesus challenged them to become great through service. In other words, He gave them a call to lead through service. When God calls us, there is no tension between our desire to lead and doing the will of God. His will is what we sincerely want to do. Also, our lives are lived fully in harmony with our destiny.

With regard to how to serve, it is important that we see what needs to be done, have a spiritual burden to do it, and then listen to the voice of the Spirit as to how to meet the need. We serve because there is a need to be met.

The Bible is replete with examples of men and women who felt called of God for specific tasks. Many of these examples of God's call are supernatural in character. It is important, however, to know that these examples stand out because of their special character. No doubt multitudes of people were called to given tasks in ways much more ordinary. We realize that God is at work even in the ordinary ways. We know that God can call today in any way that He chooses.

While we are planning our future, God directs our paths. Also, we may hear the inner voice of the Spirit. The Spirit guides us by quickening His Word, assisting us as we pray, giving us wise counsellors, using the circumstances of life, and giving spiritual gifts. The end result is that we can hear the reassuring voice of the Spirit say, "Go and fulfill your call without misgivings."

CHAPTER TWELVE
HOW TO SERVE
Introduction

The main point Jesus made in the Matthew story is that those who would be great should be your servant and those who would be first should be your slave (Matt. 20:26-27). When I read this story in the fall of 1973, I determined that this story would be the major guideline for the operation of ICI (Global University). Much later, I made the same decision for the ministry of Network211. Over the years, this story set forth for us an ideal that we wanted to achieve. How well we did it is for others to evaluate, but our desire was to serve.

As organizations, Global University and Network211 continue to meet needs. The ministries of Global University have to do with evangelism, discipleship, training of lay workers, and training of ministers. As a school, it seeks to meet the needs of individual students worldwide. Also, it seeks to meet the needs of Bible schools and of students in cooperation with the schools. Similarly, Network211 meets the spiritual needs of people worldwide through Internet evangelism and discipleship. In addition, one of its major goals is to assist local churches by helping them mount targeted evangelism campaigns. Both organizations work at home and abroad.

My purpose in this chapter, however, is not to present the programs of Global University and Network211. Rather, my purpose is to discuss the leadership principles that help organizations such as these function well. These principles tell the "inside story" of what leaders do. They tell us, in practical ways, how we can lead by serving. We are attracted by the ideal of serving, but we have to determine what this means in practical terms.

A special feature of both Global University and Network211 is that we have the privilege of working closely with and through the General Council of the Assemblies of God, including Assemblies of God World Missions (AGWM). The section in this chapter on "Working with the Leaders" highlights reaching your ministry goals through a large organization such as AGWM. However, the leadership principles can be widely applied to various situations.

We will turn now to the relevant leadership principles. I will discuss general principles of leadership, how to work with the leaders, how to work with other organizations, how to work with staff, and some guidelines for self-discipline.

General Principles

First, avoid paying too much attention to either praise or blame. It is possible that we can be unfairly praised or blamed. We should not let this deter us from following God's will. When things go well, we may be praised, but we should not allow this to make us full of pride. We know that, without God's enablement, we could not accomplish His plans for us. When things don't go well, we may be blamed. If we are to blame, we must improve and move on. We can take comfort in the fact that we did our best and follow God's leading for the future. Keep in mind that people who are either praising or blaming you can sometimes quickly change.

Second, be generous when giving credit to others. Many people feel rather unappreciated for their efforts. Special effort should be made to commend people for the good work that they do. It is wise to give credit to others whenever you can honestly do so. As a leader, you will inevitably receive some credit for the progress of your organization. Sometimes, the credit actually should go to you, and you can in all humility accept it. However, you know and should acknowledge that much credit goes to the people on your staff. The wise leader will be careful to acknowledge their contributions to your outreach.

Third, keep in tune with the times. Times change. Although our message is based on the Bible and unchanging truths, our presentation may change with the times. Our message is unchanging. With regard to methods, we usually need to change with the times. Methods move on. You have to know what is going on around you and move with the times. In some cases, it is best that you be current with the times, neither ahead nor behind. Seldom is it wise to be behind the times. Sometimes, a leader needs to be ahead of the group he leads. This enables him to lead others toward new goals. If a leader gets too far ahead, he may have to patiently pursue his goals while time catches up.

Fourth, make delay work for you. You may be delayed by people who have authority over you, by the circumstances of life, by unforeseen obstacles, and many other factors. When you experience delay, but still want to reach your goal, you can use the delay time to build a better outreach. During delay time, your worthy goals may be refined, but this only will make them more worthy. Achieving the goals will be worth the delay. Very often, as time passes, we understand better the reason for the delay. So it is best to keep our focus on the steps we need to take to improve what we are doing.

Fifth, respect everyone, but do not fear anyone. Obviously, I am talking about your colleagues, not lawless people. Within your organization, treat everyone both above you and below you on your organizational chart with respect. Also, we must respect those with whom we work who are not in our organization. Most people, including leaders, want to be respected but not feared. Good leaders in the church do not want to be feared. They know that you cannot do your best work when you are afraid. Everyone should just be courteous to each other.

Sixth, sometimes you have to lose in order to win. One of the most striking features of Christ's teaching was the paradox of "gain through loss." He taught, for example, that when people compel us to go one mile, we should go two. This is true both for organizations and for individuals. As we work with others, there will be times when we may have to "lose," but it is amazing how many times our "loss" turns to "gain." Very often we win more when we think we have lost than when we think we have won. This approach goes a step beyond the "win-win" approach that is often advocated in leadership teaching.

Working with the Leaders

This section, especially, has a twofold application. Primarily, it deals with how an international ministry can work with the leaders of the Assemblies of God World Missions (AGWM). The organization of AGWM, except for international ministries, is based on geography, so the leaders supervise geographical areas. The international ministries serve in many lands. The primary loyalty of the missionaries is to the leaders in geographical areas. However, the geographical leaders often agree to work with the leaders of the international ministries in mutually acceptable ways.

There are, of course, many organizations, including institutions, churches, and companies, that do not work through another large entity such as AGWM. Even though this section is written especially with those in mind who do, much that is said applies to organizations that do not. The leaders in every organization, whether they work through a large organization or not, have to work with people who are their leaders. Leaders of corporations, for example, work with others, such as their Board of Directors.

First, study and support your leaders. We have the privilege of working with them. In AGWM, this means working with leaders such as the Regional Directors and Area Directors. These are the geographical leaders. It is not hard to study them as their thoughts on many topics are quite well known. Usually, our leaders have some projects and policies that have priority in their minds. These priority items constitute the framework within which they work. We can work in harmony with their framework and support them even while advancing our vision. When these leaders "buy into" our vision, our cause will be greatly advanced.

Second, goals trump philosophy. It is important to know what the goals of our leaders are. Many world missions leaders hold to the philosophy of the indigenous church, but there are variations of this. The indigenous church philosophy is that the national churches ought to be self-governing, self-propagating, and self-supporting. However, each situation is different and demands its own solution. So, many of the leaders in missions are quite pragmatic in what they do. We need to know that their goals may be more important than their philosophies. When we harmonize with their views, we can make progress toward our goals.

Third, develop the philosophy for your organization. In 1969, I wrote my own philosophy of missions. This philosophy was flexible enough to allow us to work with the philosophies of the various AGWM leaders. My philosophy assumed that the national churches wanted to work cooperatively with others. So, building on the indigenous church approach, I changed self-government, self-propagation, and self-support to cooperative-autonomy, cooperative-propagation, and cooperative-support. This philosophy was flexible enough to work with the philosophies of the geographic leaders and to include the emphasis on people groups.

Fourth, approach disagreement with your leaders diplomatically. Maximize your points of agreement and think creatively about your disagreements. Most leaders will not expect you to always agree with them. Normally, leaders do not want you to be obsequious and may feel uncomfortable around those who are. Even so, how you express your disagreement does make a difference. Usually, but not always, it is best to express your differences privately. Much depends on the nature of the disagreement, the situation in which a different opinion might be expressed, and the courtesy with which you say it.

Fifth, you can win while being subordinate. Normally, you cannot win much in a confrontational way. When you are confrontational, it can call forth a like response. A better way is to submit your plans and be willing to take "no" for an answer. Many times, this can be a temporary result. You can listen to the objections that may have been raised, back off for a season, give the leaders time, and come back with a better proposal. You can bring a new proposal in a better package when you meet again. If you have listened well, you may have overcome the objections and prepared the way for approval.

Sixth, build on the basis of mutual trust. Begin by being trustworthy in all that you do. When you are trustworthy, your capacity to be trusted will be known. In addition, proceed on the assumption that your leaders are trustworthy. It has been my privilege to have a relationship built on trust with many leaders. Over time, trust builds and is a major element in your working relationships. Sometimes, something may happen that unsettles the basis of trust. Usually, in such situations, the solution is to simply clarify what has happened. If trust has been broken, then all parties will have some work to do in repairing the relationship.

Seventh, make ambiguity work for you. AGWM is a global organization that relates to national churches, other organizations, and many ministries country-by-country. Although administrative procedures are well-developed, the very nature of the work precludes having every detail well-defined. Inevitably, there will be some ambiguity in lines of authority, processes, and procedures. If you are not overly concerned about this, you can make ambiguity work for you. Most things can be worked out when colleagues are working together in trustworthy relationships. It is important, of course, to exercise good judgment concerning what to do when there is no clear policy.

Eighth, an international ministry connected with AGWM marches with the armies of other men. Many of the people who work with you have their primary loyalty with leaders over countries, regions, and territories. Your work as a leader of an international ministry crosses geographical boundaries. Although you have a staff at the home base that works directly with you, your work in other lands is with people with secondary loyalty to you and your international ministry. Thus, you are marching with the armies of other leaders. Fortunately, general patterns of operation develop over time that make it easy for everyone to work together.

Working with Other Organizations

First, find out the real interests and needs of other organizations. We work with missionary field fellowships, missions leaders, national churches, Bible schools, various ministries, and others. Each entity has its own special needs and interests. When your ministry has something that meets their needs, they may well be very interested in talking with you about working together. A lasting working relationship is always based on mutual benefit. This does not mean that other ministries are selfish. Each ministry wants to do its best to reach outreach goals and is interested in resources that will help them do this.

Second, deal with the issues of control, credit, and cash. Who controls the programs, who gets the credit, and who pays the bills are crucial issues. When you are talking over plans to work together with other entities, these issues must be dealt with sooner or later. Quite often, discussions start with other matters and gradually turn to one or more of these issues. It is normally better to openly put these points on the agenda for discussion so that all parties will know they will be discussed. When all parties are flexible on all three points, agreements can normally be worked out.

Third, share as much control as possible. Each organization will have some things that they have to control. This is normal. However, when working with other organizations, each entity should carefully determine what control they can share. Someone once said to compare the amount of sand you can hold in a tightly clinched hand versus an upturned open hand. A more open-handed approach is generally more productive. Unless it is necessary to control an aspect of your work, be willing to share control.

Fourth, make room for the brand of the other organizations. Each organization, church, or ministry is building its own brand. This is an important aspect of building an outreach. For people to find you and relate to who you are, it helps to have a name that is known. So, in working with other organizations, allow for them to make their name known. All organizations, however, have to put their brand second to what is best for the Kingdom of God. If it is better for the Kingdom of God for an entity to work silently, then that is what should be done. God will justly reward each organization for its efforts.

Fifth, have a good understanding about who is paying the bills. Quite often, the control of a ministry and the credit for it go with paying the bills. This is a fairly normal expectation. There are times, however, when an organization pays the bills without having either control of the ministry or credit for it. We sometimes say that this is giving "without strings." Any arrangement is possible, but it is important to have a good understanding of what the arrangement is. When the arrangement is made, the terms should be openly discussed and mutually accepted.

Sixth, when accreditation is desired, the standards of accreditation must be maintained. To go with control, credit, and cash, we might call this certification. All four of these issues have to be discussed. Global University has a method of working with other schools in such a way that the other schools can benefit from its accreditation. This is done largely through the materials and assessment tools that Global University has developed. The schools working with Global University have to agree to administer all the programs in a suitable way. Most schools find that the standards are reasonable and can be maintained.

Working with Staff

First, lead your team by example. This is especially important in an organization that has a lot of volunteer workers and personnel who get their support somewhere else. Most of these workers are totally committed to their work, but it is appropriate for them to expect the same commitment from you as the leader. So, it is important that you lead by example. There may be some workers who will be a little less committed than you are. For example, they may get to work a bit later than you do and perhaps leave earlier. In contrast, some workers will do more. They deserve our commendation and gratitude.

Second, match motivation with ministry gifts. When enlisting new workers, find out what motivates them and what their ministry gifts are. Try to assign them to a task that matches their motivation and ministry gifts. If they want to perform given tasks and have the ability, much can be accomplished. In some cases, making this match is just not possible. In such cases, you have to depend on workers doing their best at tasks that are not in harmony with their primary gifts. Many times, fortunately, this can be a temporary assignment. Obviously, people do their best work when their motivation and ministry gifts match their roles.

Third, build on the strengths of each person. Every person has strengths and weaknesses. Usually, these are well known to both peers and leaders. Whenever possible, build on strengths, not the weaknesses. We may have to build on potential strengths. This building can begin with training for the needed role. We may not be able to overcome some of the weaknesses that people have, but we can have them do what they are, at least, potentially gifted to do. Hopefully, the strengths of each worker will match the needed roles. Building on strengths is a good way to maximize the efforts of the staff.

Fourth, surround a problem person with positive action. You may have problems with a person on your staff. You can overcome the problem by surrounding it with positive actions and people that make the case moot. For example, if a person is not happy with his role, you can listen carefully to his complaint and begin to think of what role might be more suitable. At the same time, you can make sure that people around him are positive in their outlook. It is not always possible to turn such a person around, but it is often very helpful to try. When you are successful, you can gain the results produced by the worker.

Fifth, turn moments of conflict into creative sessions. Some conflict is not only inevitable in any organization, but it is often good. When conflict cannot be resolved, it can be harmful. Whether it is resolved or not depends, in part, on how you approach it. It is wise to allow everyone at the table to speak their minds on a given issue. Assuming this is led properly, it can be done without a lot of discord and emotion. The next step is to posit creative alternatives that everyone can accept. Sometimes, but not always, you will be rewarded with great new ideas. These new ideas can spur your organization on to greater deeds.

Self-Discipline

First, know your own vision. It is important to define your own vision and do it in a way that can be simply communicated. Until the vision is clear, you will not gain a lot of support. Many times, people begin a new work with a vision that is not well-defined. When this is the case, the leader with the vision must devote time and effort to refining his vision. This often takes a lot of consultation with others as well as interaction with potential followers. The work of the visionary in defining the vision is not done until it can be simply stated in very understandable terms. We live in an era of sound bites when "concise" and "clear" are the watchwords.

Second, keep your eye on the ball. Every leader of a ministry needs to know what his vision and mission is. Also, he needs to keep his focus and attention on the ministry he supervises. Just keep your eye on the ball that you are supposed to hit.

Every ministry leader has opportunities to do things that are not related to the ministry's vision and mission. Although new things inevitably will be done, they should be done in harmony with the vision and mission. Or, as an alternative, the vision and mission can be modified to fit the new scope of the ministry. Everyone on the staff should know and subscribe to the vision.

Third, mind your own business. The temptation, when working in an organization such as AGWM, is to be sidetracked into commenting on issues unrelated to your main tasks. You should not spend time and energy getting involved pro and con in other issues. You may have an opinion, but do not need to express it. For example, because the business on the floor of the General Council does not have much to do with missionaries, they usually do not comment on the business. On some occasions, you may be called upon to express an opinion, but it is not your primary job to monitor others.

Fourth, always be secure. At times, leaders may suffer from a sense of insecurity. When this happens, the entire organization suffers. When you are secure, you can handle the problems that come your way. The secure leader does not worry about his status, his understanding of the ministry, and his ability to do the job. Neither is he insecure about colleagues that may test his leadership. A sense of security comes from focusing on God and His Kingdom, not on yourself. When you are secure, others around you feel secure. An organization filled with secure people can accomplish much with joy in so doing.

Fifth, be realistic, not cynical. There will always be the temptation to be cynical about an organization and leaders you work with. Even strong leaders can become cynical about the leaders of the larger entity with which they may work. In any entity, there will be events or actions that could call forth a cynical response. However, the better response is just to be realistic. Most people, for example, act many times in their own interest or with mixed motivation. It is a bonus when they go beyond their interests and engage in altruistic activity. We should not be cynical about it.

Sixth, keep the faith. Leading is a daily walk of faith. We must move with the conviction that we are in God's will and that He will meet every need. Even when the days seem dark, let the light of faith shine in our hearts. Most ministry leaders face the challenge of raising the funds for their ministries. This is always a challenging task. In addition, the walk of faith includes God's supply of personnel, people to make talented contributions to the work, the overall harmony of the people at work, and the general health of the organization. The leader fosters a walk of faith on the part of each individual working with him.

Seventh, make prayer and praise a vital part of your spiritual life. We must pray always that we will know the will of God and have the courage to do it. Obviously, we have special times set aside for prayer, but every moment of our lives can be saturated with praise and prayer. Even while we are busy at work, our attitude can be expressive of our heart for God. Our prayers and praises are expressions of our submission to God and our dependency upon Him. When we pray, we work together with God to accomplish His purposes.

Eighth, make the will of God the supreme force in your life. For example, it is more important to pray that we are in God's will than to pray for finances to do His will. Clearly, we have to do both, but when we focus on His will, He will take care of the rest of our concerns. Knowing the will of God for us is a major element in our leadership. When we are convinced that we are in the will of God, great faith is born, and a sense of confidence settles over us. We know that God will enable us to do what He wants us to do. Moreover, we will continue to grow in the image of Christ and become like Him in all our ways.

Ninth, we must be led by the Spirit. One of the outstanding characteristics of the leaders of the early church was that they were led by the Spirit in what they did. For example, when Peter set out to go to the house of Cornelius with the men who came to his house, he said, "The Spirit told me to go with them without misgivings" (Acts 11:12). When we know that the Spirit is leading, we can have the deep assurance that we are doing God's work in God's way. When we have this inner assurance, we can act with confidence. Armed with this faith and confidence, we can watch God at work unfolding His purposes in the world.

Conclusion

The emphasis of this chapter is on how we can serve. Jesus told us that we can become great through service. The principles given above describe for us what this means inside an organization that works within the framework of a larger organization such as AGWM. However, many of the principles discussed apply to entities that do not work through a larger organization.

It is amazing to me how much truth Christ taught in such concise form. The story in Matthew 20:20-28 is a prime example. This story raises at least the issues discussed in this book. Many organizations are confronted with these issues and will be able to join the discussion of them. In addition, the story provides a basis for principles that make an organization run smoothly as well as how one organization can work within a larger organization on a harmonious basis. The summation of it all is that we are all at our best when we are meeting the felt and real needs of the people that we serve.

SCRIPTURE INDEX

BIBLIOGRAPHY

Books

Alexander, John W. *Managing Our Work*. Downers Grove: Inter-Varsity Press, 1972.

Allen, R. Earl. *Bible Paradoxes*. Fleming H. Revell Company, Westwood, 1963.

Barna, George. *Leaders on Leadership*. Ventura: Regal, 1997.

Barnes, Albert. *Notes on the New Testament: Matthew and Mark*. Grand Rapids: Baker Book House, 1987 Reprint.

Bauer, Walter. *A Greek-English Lexicon of the New Testament and Other Early Christian Literature*. Fourth Revised and Augmented Edition, 1952. Chicago: The University of Chicago Press, 1957.

Blackaby, Henry and Richard. *Spiritual Leadership: Moving People to God's Agenda*. Nashville: B & H Publishing Group, 2011.

Blanchard, Ken and Phil Hodges. *Lead Like Jesus*. Nashville: W. Publishing Group, 2005.

Bogardus, Emory S. *Leaders and Leadership*. New York: Appleton-Century-Crofts, Inc., 1934.

Bruce, F. F. *Commentary on the Book of Acts*. Grand Rapids: Wm. B. Eerdmans Publishing Co., 1954.

Burge, Gary M. General Editor: Terry Mack. *The Letters of John: The NIV Application Commentary*. Grand Rapids: Zondervan, 1996.

Carnegie, Dale. *How to Win Friends and Influence People*. New York: Simon and Schuster, 1936.

Chappell, Clovis G. *The Seven Words*. New York: Abingdon Press, 1952.

Clinton, J. Robert. *The Making of a Leader*. Colorado Springs: Navpress, 1988.

Cummings, Robert W. *Gethsemane*. Springfield: Gospel Publishing House, 1944.

Dean, Ed and Drexel T. Brunson. *The Servant Organization for Jesus*. Amazon.com, 2013.

Drucker, Peter F. *The Effective Executive*. London: Pan Books Ltd., 1967.

_____. *Managing the Non-Profit Organization*. New York: Harper Business, 1990.

Erdman, Charles R. *The Gospel of Matthew*. Philadelphia: The Westminster Press, 1948.

Erickson, Millard J. *Christian Theology*. Grand Rapids: Baker Book House, 1983.

Finzel, Hans. *Empowered Leaders*. Nashville: Word Publishers, 1998.

Fisher, James L. *Power of the Presidency*. New York: Macmillan Publishing Company, 1984.

Flattery, George M. Doctoral Thesis: "*A Comparative Analysis of Herman Harrell Horne's Idealistic Philosophy of education and the Philosophy of Religious Education reflected in the Adult Curriculum of the Assemblies of God (1959-1964)*" Fort Worth: Southwestern Baptist Theological Seminary, 1966.

Gangel, Kenneth O. General Editor: Max Anders. *Holman New Testament Commentary: Acts*. Nashville: 1998.

Gibb, Cecil A. "Leadership," in Gardner Lindzey, ed., *Handbook of Social Psychology*. Cambridge, Mass.: Addison-Wesley Publishing Company, 1954.

Glasser, William. *Reality Therapy*. New York: Harper and Row, 1965.

Greenleaf, Robert K. *Servant Leadership: A Journey into the Nature of Legitimate Power and Greatness*. 25th Anniversary Edition. Mahwah: Paulist Press, 2002

Harris, Thomas A. *I'm OK-You're OK*. New York: Avon Publishers, 1969.

Hendriksen, William. *New Testament Commentary: Exposition of the Gospel of Matthew*. Grand Rapids: Baker Book House, 1973.

Hesse, Hermann. Trans. by Hilda Rosner. *Journey to the East*. New York: Picador, 1956.

Hunter, James C. *The World's Most Powerful Leadership Principle*: *How to Become a Servant Leader*. New York: Crown Business, 2004.

Kennedy, John F. *Profiles in Courage*. New York: Harper and Brothers, 1956.

Korda, Michael. *Power! How to Get It, How to Use It*. New York: Ballantine Books, 1975.

Kouzes, James M. and Barry Z. Posner. *The Leadership Challenge*. San Francisco, Jossey-Bass Publishers, 1995.

Kraft, Charles H. *I Give You Authority*. Grand Rapids: Chosen Books, 1997.

151

Lamsa, George M. *The Holy Bible from Ancient and Eastern Manuscripts*. Philadelphia: A. J. Holman Company, 1957.

Lenski, R. C. H. *St. Matthew's Gospel*. Columbus: The Wartburg Press, 1943.

Lyon, R. W. *Evangelical Theological Dictionary*, ed. Elwell, Walter A. Grand Rapids: Baker Book House, 1984.

Maxwell, John C. *Developing the Leader within You*. Nashville: Thomas Nelson Publishers, 1993.

Morris, Leon. J. D. Douglas, Organizing Editor. *New Bible Dictionary*, Second Edition. Wheaton: Tyndale House Publishers, 1982.

_____. *The Atonement*. Downers Grove: Inter-Varsity Press, 1983.

Packer, J. I. *Evangelism and the Sovereignty of God*. London: Inter-Varsity Fellowship, 1961.

Robertson, A. T. *Word Pictures in the New Testament*. Nashville: Broadman Press, 1930.

Ross, Murray G. and Charles E. Hendry. *New Understandings of Leadership*. New York: Association Press, 1957.

Sanders, J. Oswald. *Spiritual Leadership*. Chicago: Moody Press, 1967.

Shostrom, Everett L. *Man, the Manipulator*. New York: Bantam Books, 1968.

Stagg, Frank. Matthew. Henry E. Turlington. Mark. General Editor: Clifton J. Allen. *The Broadman Bible Commentary: Matthew-Mark*. Nashville: The Broadman Press, 1969.

Tead, Ordway. *The Art of Leadership*. New York: McGraw-Hill Book Company, Inc., 1935.

Titus, Charles Hickman. *The Processes of Leadership*. Dubuque: Wm. C. Brown Company, 1950.

Tozer, A. W. *The Pursuit of God*. Harrisburg: Christian Publications, Inc., 1948.

Van Yperen, Jim. General Editor: George Barna. *"Conflict: The Refining Fire of Leadership."* Ventura: Regal, 1997.

Vine, W. E., Merrill R. Unger, and William White Jr. *Vine's Complete Expository Dictionary of Old and New Testament Words*. Nashville: Thomas Nelson, 1996.

Wolff, Richard. *Man at the Top*. Wheaton: Tyndale House Publishers, 1970.

Articles and Journals

Bits and Pieces. (April, 1973)

Bits and Pieces (July, 1973)

Bits and Pieces. (June 25, 1992)

Bits and Pieces (April 30, 1992)

Gibb, Cecil A. "The Principles and Traits of Leadership," *Journal of Abnormal and Social Psychology* (Vol. 42, 1947, 272).

Hutchinson, John C. "Servanthood: Jesus' Countercultural Call to Christian Leaders." *Bibliotheca Sacra* 166 (January-March 2009: 53-69).

Maslow, A. H. "A Theory of Human Motivation," *Psychological Review*, L. No 4 (1943), 370-396.

Smart, James D. "Mark 10:35-45." *Interpretation*, (Vol. 33: no. 3, July 1979, 288-293).

Web Sites

Emerson, Ralph Waldo.
http://thinkexist.com/quotation/every_great_institution_is_the_lengthened_shadow/224721.html .

Koltko-Rivera, Mark E. "Rediscovering the Later Version of Maslow's Hierarchy of Needs: Self-Transcendence and Opportunities for Theory, Research, and Unification." Retrieved from http://academic.udayton.edu/jackbauer/Readings%20595/Koltko-Rivera%2006%20trans%20self-act%20copy.pdf .

McLeod, S. A. (2007, 2016). "Maslow's Hierarchy of Needs." Retrieved from www.simplypsychology.org/maslow.html .

Morrison, Robert. (May 10, 2011) "I Felt as if I Were Walking with Destiny" Winston Churchill.
http://www.americanthinker.com/articles/2011/05/i_felt_as_if_i_were_walking_wi.html .

Roosevelt, Theodore.
http://thinkexist.com/quotation/no_man_is_worth_his_salt_who_is_not_ready_at_all/193866.html .

Made in the USA
Middletown, DE
15 January 2017